Realism, Myth, and History in Defoe's Fiction

Laetitia Atkins; vulgarly call'd Moll Flanders

Realism, Myth, and History in Defoe's Fiction

Maximillian E. Novak

University of Nebraska Press   Lincoln and London 1983

Frontispiece from an edition of MOLL FLANDERS *published in 1776 by F. Noble and T. Lowndes. It was renamed* THE HISTORY OF LAETITIA ATKINS VULGARLY CALLED MOLL FLANDERS *and said to have been taken from Defoe's original manuscript.*

Publication of this book was assisted by a grant from the National Endowment for the Humanities.

Portions of this book have previously been published in different form as "Crime and Punishment in *Roxana*," *JEPG* 65 (1966): 445–65; "Defoe's Indifferent Monitor," *ECS* 3 (1970): 351–65; "History, Ideology, and the Method of Defoe's Historical Fiction," *Studies in the Eighteenth Century* (Canberra, 1979), pp. 79–141; "The Imaginative Genesis of *Robinson Crusoe*," *Tennessee Studies in Literature* 19 (1974): 57–58; and "The Literature of Crime as a Narrative System (1660–1842)," *Yearbook of English Studies* (Leeds, 1981), 11:29–48.

Library of Congress Cataloging in Publication Data
Novak, Maximillian E.
Realism, myth, and history in Defoe's fiction.
Includes bibliographical references and index.
1. Defoe, Daniel, 1667?–1731—Criticism and interpretation. I. Title.
PR3407.N68 1983   823'.5   82–11141
ISBN 0–8032–3307–8

For Estelle, Ralph, Daniel, and Rachel

Contents

Illustrations

Preface

. . . any body who can relish Words, may be very positive by the Arch Waggery therein, it was wrote by D——l D——e, when awaked, and that when in a Deep Sleep he wrote his Remarks, or at least was tyed up from his usual merry waggish way of Joke and Pun by those who hired him. REMARKS UPON REMARKS (*London, n.d. [ca. 1725]*), *p. viii.*

THE ANONYMOUS AUTHOR of the above comment was neither an enemy nor a supporter of Defoe. Indeed, by 1725, the bitterness that had been aroused by the political wars of the reigns of William III, Queen Anne, and the early years of George I had faded somewhat, and there was a lull before the violent attacks on Walpole's government initiated by the *Craftsman* at the end of 1726. The writer of *Remarks upon Remarks* thought he knew that Defoe might write on any side of an issue and wondered if he might have had a hand in the works he was discussing. He was certainly wrong, but what he thought of when he raised the possibility of Defoe's authorship was word play and humor, or "Waggery." The Defoe that he knew was not so much the controversial journalist, political theorist, and projector but rather the novelist, biographer of criminals, and witty writer of periodical essays of the reign of George I. When literary historians think of Defoe's reputation, they tend to recall Swift's sneering pretense at having forgotten Defoe's name, or Pope's image of Defoe raised on high in the pillory above the other Dunces, but as Dr. Johnson remarked, anyone forming an opinion about the first half of the eighteenth century through the opinions of Pope and Swift would have a distorted view of their contemporaries and the events of the time.

Indeed, the first substantial treatment of Defoe's career in "Cibber's" *Lives of the Poets* (1753), twenty-one years after his death, dismissed the opinions of the Scriblerians out of hand: "De Foe can never, with any propriety, be ranked amongst the dunces; for whoever reads his works with candour and impartiality, must be convinced that he was a man of the strongest natural powers, a lively imagination, and solid judgment, which, joined with an unshaken probity in his moral conduct, and an invincible integrity in the political sphere, ought not only to screen him from the petulant attacks of satire, but transmit his name with some degree of applause to posterity."[1] Whatever may be said about this writer's opinion of Defoe's political integrity, his highly favorable judgment on Defoe was to go unchallenged during the following decades until, by 1830, Defoe became a saint and martyr in the cause of free enterprise and Whig principles of politics in Walter Wilson's extensive biography. Another interesting aspect of the life in "Cibber's" *Lives* is the inclusion of a brief bibliography with such anonymous pieces as *A Journal of the Plague Year, Colonel Jack,* and *The Complete English Tradesman.* While it would be difficult to prove, a case could be made for a substantial audience during the 1720s that recognized and appreciated Defoe's writings and for a continued awareness of his productions throughout the century.

This is not to deny that most of the discussions of Defoe by his contemporaries were in the nature of vicious attacks associating him with the new and terrifying power of an anonymous journalism. As one of his enemies wrote,

Great Bulzebube himself he does outvie,
For Malice, Treachery, and Audacious Lye.
Behold what Crimes lye in his Conscious Breast,
Legions of Devils this Mans Soul to poss'd.[2]

But there was also a small chorus of praise, and one attack shows Defoe in the midst of his admirers.[3] On the whole, it may be said that he was always considered a writer of great talent and force. However different they were in their opinions, Defoe shared with his brilliant contemporaries, Swift and Pope, the power that liter-

ary genius gave to men in the early eighteenth century. He could
say with Pope:

> Yes, I am proud; I must be proud to see
> Men not afraid of God, afraid of me:
> Safe from the Bar, the Pulpit, and the Throne,
> Yet touch'd and sham'd by *Ridicule* alone.[4]

In this study of Defoe, I do not intend to apologize for his
occasional inaccuracies and lapses into mediocrity. Rather I treat
him as one of the great writers of his time and attempt to locate
his excellence in his genius as a creator of fictions and in the
often–underestimated complexities of his style and language. In
so doing, I have chosen to concentrate on a limited number of his
major works, being content to have made a point with, say, *Moll
Flanders,* that would only be repeated in any separate examination
of *Captain Singleton* or *Colonel Jack.* By way of treating the individual works, I have attempted to move from an examination of
Defoe's writings and their contemporary background to larger
questions concerning his artistry and influence. In the first chapter I attempt to establish the theoretical grounds for Defoe's realism, for his creation of mythic patterns of action and character,
and for his use of narrative. The second chapter treats *Robinson
Crusoe* as his most imaginative fiction and as a book that, in its
island experience, is at once divorced from history and yet rooted
in the daily events appearing in Defoe's journalism of the years
prior to 1719, the time of its publication. A discussion of Defoe's
two major historical fictions and his methods of shaping history
to suit his narrative purposes constitutes the material of the next
chapter. The fourth section deals with Moll Flanders as a character who appears at first to fit into the pattern of criminal biography and the fictional adventures of female roguery. But I attempt
to demonstrate the ways in which Defoe's narrative questions the
nature of his protagonist's experiences in a manner that was entirely original. In the following chapter on *Roxana,* Defoe's most
complex fiction, I try to use all the methods of the former chapters
to trace the historical sources for Defoe's mythic "fortunate mistress" and to examine the moral significance of her thoughts and
actions. The final chapter treats Defoe's role in infusing particular
attitudes toward crime into accounts of the lives of criminals and

in shaping the part crime was to play in future fiction. The entire book constitutes a speculative study of Defoe's imagination as it fused the events of history with the materials of fantasy into a unique type of fiction.

Although I can lay claim to some singlemindedness in my attempt to explore Defoe's fictive imagination, I do not want to pretend to a unified methodology. My main concern was to find ways of explaining why Defoe's fiction remains so effective over a period of two and a half centuries while the writings of some other novelists, perhaps more highly praised in their time than Defoe was in his, now appear imprisoned in the fictional conventions of their periods. Formalist methods have not always been the most rewarding in treating Defoe, but I began by trying to determine the nature of the genres in which Defoe was working, whether older forms or those shaped by his creative genius. While this remained a point of departure in examining each novel, I soon found that explanations based on genre, as much as they might indicate certain directions, did not seem to answer most of my questions. Genre is an important issue throughout my discussions, but I have preferred to think more in terms of modes—an organizational principle that includes social and historical contexts as well as formal constructions. And in treating *Robinson Crusoe* and *Moll Flanders*, I have tried to explain the responses to these works over the centuries in a manner that is almost directly contrary to considerations of genre. Similarly, in my final chapter, while attempting to define various kinds of writings on crime, I have tried to draw from an impossible conflation of forms some themes crucial to that particular line in the history of fiction concerned with matters of guilt and criminality.

I have tried to keep within terminology that is not far removed from Defoe's own language. For example, I will refer to history as an account of past events rooted in fact, dates, and actions. Defoe once referred to his journalism as equivalent to writing history "by Inches."[5] I use the term *myth* for those kinds of fictions that tend away from the specificity of history toward general ideas, actions, and characters. When I speak of fictions, I mean any kind of narrative or narrative situation, however brief; my tendency is to focus on short episodes in larger fictions. When I use the term *novel*, it will be in the neutral sense of a sustained narrative of several hundred pages. When I want to refer to the traditional novel as practiced by Jane Austen and George Eliot, I will use the distinction suggested by Northrop Frye and call it the "novel of manners."[6]

No one can write on Defoe without drawing on some of the splendid criticism and scholarship of this century. For example, all of us writing on Defoe owe a major debt to James Sutherland, whose biography of Defoe always provides a judicious and balanced view of Defoe's character and the events of his life. His critical study of Defoe suggested some new directions for several sections of this book. And I am also obliged to the late John Robert Moore not only for the help he gave me over the years in answering my queries, but also for some of his wonderful discoveries that, by expanding the Defoe canon, also expanded the reach of Defoe's genius. I owe a particular debt to Ian Watt. Edward Hooker started me off on Defoe by suggesting that I ought to read Professor Watt's "Robinson Crusoe as a Myth." In arguing against some of his conclusions in that essay and in his brilliant *Rise of the Novel*, I have never acknowledged the degree to which his work has furnished me with the contexts for formulating my objections. From the writings of Spiro Peterson, Benjamin Boyce, Samuel Monk, and Alan McKillop I have taken innumerable suggestions. And in a somewhat different context I am obliged to G. S. Starr, J. Paul Hunter, and Ralph Rader for arguing in such a forceful manner positions with which I could not agree and which compelled me to work harder at thinking out my own views. In recent years I have reviewed the work of John Richetti, Everett Zimmerman, and David Blewett, and while I think that I had most of my ideas formulated before their work appeared, I share a variety of viewpoints with them. Finally, like all scholars working on Defoe, I have made continual use of Arthur W. Secord's edition of the *Review* and of George H. Healey's edition of the *Letters*. I had the pleasure of meeting both before their death and gained from them the sense of being part of a succession of the few at that time who knew just how good a writer Defoe was.

Grants from the Research Committee of the University of California, Los Angeles, enabled me to carry out much of the work on this volume. A research grant from the National Endowment for the Humanities allowed me to travel to England to use the inexhaustible materials at the British Library and Bodleian Library. I also want to thank the staff of the William Andrews Clark Memorial Library who furnished me with books, information, and company during the writing and research on this book. Sections of my work, usually in different form, have appeared in *Eighteenth-Century Studies*, the *Journal of English and Germanic Philology*, *Studies in the Eighteenth Century*, *Tennessee Studies in Literature*, and the *Yearbook of English Studies*. The latter essay is being reprinted by permission of the editors—G. K. Hunter and C. J. Rawson—and the Modern Humanities Research Association, publisher of the journal. Early versions of some of these essays were read before meetings of the Modern Language Association, the International Association of Professors of English, the D. Nichol Smith Seminar, and the American Society for Eighteenth-Century Studies and before audiences at the Universities of Minnesota and Wisconsin. I benefited from the questions raised at these presentations and attempted to answer some of them in my final version. Finally, I want to thank Professor Michael Seidel of Columbia University and Professor Everett Zimmerman of the University of California, Santa Barbara, for their careful reading of my manuscript and their helpful suggestions.

Realism, Myth, and History in Defoe's Fiction

1

Some Elements of Defoe's Fiction:
Realism, Myth, History, and Story

It is observ'd by the Curious, that the most difficult thing in the Limners Art is, to represent a Person singing; suppose it be the picture of a young Lady, the utmost he can do is, to shew her Countenance bright, the Company listening, and appearing pleased; but alas towards the Sound, towards the Charm of her Voice, and the Beauty of her Judgment, he can do no more than paint her with her Mouth open, which is the meanest Posture she can, with Decency, be shewn in; and unless the other Passions discover it, she may as well be supposed to be swearing, scolding, sick, or anything else, as well as singing.
DEFOE, *A Continuation of Letters Written by a Turkish Spy at Paris*[1]

SEVERAL DECADES ago, a critic remarked that Daniel Defoe "is perhaps a unique example of a great writer who was very little interested in literature, and says nothing of interest about it as literature."[2] Were this entirely true, it would be "unique" indeed, but the passage from the preface to his *Continuation of the Letters of a Turkish Spy* suggests that Defoe had more than a little curiosity about the methods by which a perceived scene might be transformed into a work of art.[3] Defoe is interested in representing the scene accurately, but since it is that of a person singing, since the sense appealed to is vision and the subject that of hearing, how is the painter to convey what cannot be achieved in the medium at hand? A person depicted with her mouth open is likely to look silly, no matter how beautiful the sound she is making may be in real life. No satisfactory solution is provided. The listeners may be shown in such a way as to suggest their pleasure; she may be depicted with her "Countenance bright." But only a total context can give a hint of the beauty of an unheard sound. Elsewhere Defoe retold the story of the painter Xeuxis who destroyed a painting of a boy holding grapes when some birds tried to eat the fruit. While some witnesses protested that the action of the birds was a compliment to his realistic depiction of the scene, Xeuxis pointed out that had the boy been as well done, the birds would not have had the temerity to come so near.[4]

In both instances, the problem involves a total context of reality. In the first example, Defoe seems to suggest that art must work indirectly by revealing the passions—passions that may not yield to paint or pencil. As a writer, a user of words, Defoe often tried to achieve the vividness of the painter, but one of his standard effects is to have his narrators confess that they are unable to depict a scene accurately. Sometimes it is a scene from which they turn away and refuse to describe. At other times the scene is so horrible or involves such emotions that the viewer finds himself lost for words. As a skilled writer, Defoe was seldom at a loss for words. In one of those issues of the *Review* in which he speculated on effective writing, Defoe remarked:

If I understand what is the general Acceptation of the Word as it relates to Authors, a Man is called Dull, when there appears no Spirit, no Relish or Vivacity, in what he Writes; when his Stile does not touch, when the Clearness and Perspicuity of his Expressions, the happy Turn in his Relation, the fineness and Politeness of his Stile, the Cadence and Musick of his Words, does not touch the Reader, surprize his Fancy, and fire his Imagination as he expects.[5]

This may seem an odd kind of statement from a writer who has often been accused of having a simple homely style, but in his own time many readers considered Defoe the liveliest writer on the literary scene.[6]

What gave him this reputation was the element of narrative, often fanciful narrative, in his writings. In the following pages I intend to explore the nature of that narrative, the ways in which it succeeded in moving his readers. I want to re-examine the character of Defoe's realism, to explore the patterns by which Defoe managed to create entire worlds of fiction, and to investigate his notion of the story itself as a means of communicating. Throughout this study I have treated narratives, whether based in history or purely fictional, whether woven into what we think of now as novel-length fiction or standing as a brief example in didactic works, in more or less the same manner. Defoe's fanatical churchman of *The Shortest Way with the Dissenters* may not be the subject of a novel, but he plays his role in that brief pamphlet with as much conviction as a character in a work of fiction. It is the variety of Defoe's methods that interests me here rather than their unity, and I begin with one of the most traditional in writings on Defoe—his realism.

I

When it was growing and grown, I have observ'd already, how many things I wanted, to Fence it, Secure it, Mow or Reap it, Cure and Carry it Home, Thrash, Part it from the Chaff, and Save it. Then I wanted a Mill to Grind it, Sieves to Dress it, Yeast and Salt to make it into Bread, and an Oven to bake it, and yet all these things I did without, as shall be observed. DEFOE, *Robinson Crusoe*[7]

All these things the good old man gave Money to his Wife to provide; and these pretty things together amounted to a great sum. But all of them was nothing considerable to her next demand, and that was a Cup-boards-head of Plate; some there was in the house, viz. a beerbowl, a Beaker, a Salt, and a dozen of Apostle Spoons: but these must be changed, and others provided; viz. one large Tanckard, two smaller of an equal size, one Plate, one Sugar-dish, two or three Porringers, two Caudle-Cups, two dozen of Spoons, a couple of Candlesticks, one pair of Snuffers; and such a large Inventory of this kind of Ware she did reckon up, that it troubled her Husband, and almost broke his heart to think how to satisfie the ambitious humour of his Wife. RICHARD HEAD AND FRANCIS KIRKMAN, *The English Rogue*[8]

A quarter of a century has passed since Ian Watt's landmark study, *The Rise of the Novel*, was first published. Watt's book was written with great intellectual force and equal critical power, and it is hardly surprising that it has become the orthodox way of reading the events that followed the immense popularity of fictional narrative since that momentous day, the twenty-fifth day of April, when *Robinson Crusoe* first appeared. The originality of Watt's work is there for anyone to see. He blended discussions of social change in the eighteenth century, particularly matters involving the isolation of the individual in the city and the growth of leisure, with information about the price of books, literacy, contemporary theories in philosophy concerning the nature of reality or of identity, and discussions of names in fiction and real life. Although Defoe had always appeared as a precursor of Richardson and Fielding, Watt gave him equal space if not equal weight with the acknowledged masters of the early novel in England. And Watt's tendency to fault Fielding for an uneven sense of realism tended to throw great importance on Defoe's mastery of the novel's realistic surface. Watt had much to criticize in Defoe, especially the inaccuracies and inconsistencies that seemed to disqualify him from any claims to careful artistry, but there is no doubt that he is responsible for the modern critical reassessment of Defoe that has firmly established him as one of the great writers of the eighteenth century.

There was so much that was new in Watt's book that only time has enabled us to see how traditional the basic fabric of it was. For example, the division of Defoe as the master of "formal realism" and Richardson of "psychological realism" owed much to Auerbach's division between the kind of realism in Homer as opposed to the inner reality to be discovered in the New Testament.[9] Watt also absorbed from Auerbach and socialist critics like Ralph Fox the sense that realism in fiction was an inherent value.[10] Wayne Booth remarks this aspect of Watt's work and questions the degree to which it will bear close scrutiny. After quoting Watt's statement that "the accurate transcription of actuality does not necessarily produce a work of any real truth or enduring literary value" and his denial that "the greater the 'formal realism' the better the work," Booth insists that "Watt's constant criterion is the achievement of realism."[11] Since many poor novels have been written in a realistic mode, the important question is, What distinguishes works of realism or what makes the reality in one novel vivid and that in another dull and dreary?

Other traditional elements in Watt's book were his tendency to treat literary history in terms of the evolution of forms and to limit himself to events happening in Great Britain. From the mid-nineteenth century forward, the history of fiction was treated as if it were some particular animal that had progressed from a primitive condition to the high point of form and structure discoverable in numerous contemporary examples. Whereas John Dunlop, in his *History of Fiction*, (1814) had accepted various forms, now the only acceptable one was the novel. Thus, the curriculum in the United States often included Scott's *Heart of Midlothian* and Dickens's *Great Expectations* not so much for their intrinsic excellence as for their more nearly resembling, in their structure, the main line of evolution to be discovered in novel form. Although Watt's own tastes lead him to appreciate the realism of Defoe and Richardson, the notion of a realism of assessment in Fielding has some connotation of a type of realism that goes beyond that to be discovered in the earlier novelists.

When Northrop Frye suggested that fiction might better be divided into four basic types: confessions, romance, anatomy, and novel (the latter in the sense of a novel of manners), he provided a break with the tradition in which Watt was still working.[12] Frye did not pretend to be tracing a historical pattern, but his categories, in their attempt to take in all fictions, were more descriptive of the actual flow of fiction in any age. The return of the picaresque as a viable form for modern fiction and the decline of the novel of manners could hardly be explained in the context provided by Earnest Baker in his encyclopedic study of the novel published at the beginning of this century. Watt's tendency to focus on fiction as if the terms of its progress were already established undermined his work as a literary history for fiction in the first half of the eighteenth century.

Also somewhat odd was the location of the inventors of the novel in Great Britain when, during the seventeenth and eighteenth centuries, France was the country famous for its prose fiction. Diana Spearman remarks that Ian Watt's dismissal of *La Princesse de Clèves* as a work outside the limits of the novel is "courageous," but she quickly adds that it is also incomprehensible. She quotes his dismissal on grounds that despite "all its psychological penetration and literary skill, we feel it to be too stylish to be authentic," rages against such an "absurd" judgment, and remarks: "Once Mme de La Fayette had written a novel of psychological analysis, even though it was about great personages, it did not require much effort of the imagination to compose a similar story set in another social situation."[13]

If Spearman considered Watt's formulation an insult to French fiction, she might equally (and indeed does) claim some precedence for Spanish contributions. To ignore *Don Quixote* as lacking in the kind of reality that the novel was to develop may be consistent with Watt's thesis, but in works of the picaresque, like *Marcos de Obregón* or *Estevanillo Gonsalez,* there are real characters with perfectly common names moving through a real landscape. And Watt ignores the popularity of both *Lazarillo de Tormes* and *The Spanish Rogue.* By the end of the seventeenth century, Mateo Alemán's mixture of fiction and moral discourse had been stripped of its ethical and religious reflections and converted into a picaresque novel with a major influence. In addition to such well-known fictions, works like *The Spanish Polecat* and *Lavernae* provided as much realistic fiction with a Spanish setting as any English reader might desire.

But while these objections are important, perhaps the greatest problem with *The Rise of the Novel* lies in the area of its most significant achievement. For while the discussion of contemporary social developments, such as a growing sense of isolation in an expanding Georgian London, may provide a background for *Robinson Crusoe* and *Moll Flanders,* such a homology between external developments and fictional events is almost impossible to prove. Because Watt is so plausible in his arguments and intelligent in his examples, the relationships seem to hold together. Yet it would be difficult to prove that there is any connection between what happens to Crusoe and Moll, to Pamela and Clarissa, and the sociological changes sketched out. *Pamela* was considered a work of fiction that embodied a clear and acceptable moral lesson. It was the first work of its kind that contemporary moralists could applaud. As such, its popularity may have had more to do with religious attitudes of the time than with any particular socioeconomic event. And the gathering of Crusoe's harvest for the making of bread may have delighted those who were still closely associated with that kind of labor as much as it did those in the city who no longer had to make their own bread at home. Such gaps between general events and the production of a work of fiction are inevitable, and Watt's arguments on these issues may be taken as suggestive rather than conclusive. Although it is those suggestions that make the book most attractive, the parts of his book to which critics usually refer are the most traditional. This is why *The Rise of the Novel* tended to harden already existing views of the novel rather than to open up new approaches.

In fact, the novel did not rise so much as it lurched in various directions, picking up new techniques and losing some that were equally valuable. The French novel and short Spanish tales that had replaced the long romances in popularity were easily available for little money. Richard Bentley published twenty volumes of such works, each containing four or five separate pieces, in 1692. There were English imitations as well, the best known of which was Congreve's *Incognita*. An English version of Spanish picaresque literature, *The English Rogue,* by Richard Head and Francis Kirkman, was influenced by the libertine spirit of English comedy in the 1670s during which it was written. If the rogues whose tales interweave through the four parts of this work are almost indistinguishable even in their sexual differences, the settings are fairly vivid. Although the detailed formal realism of some sections, such as that quoted at the head of this section, serves an almost parodic role, in other places the realism exists mainly for the sake of concreteness. Defoe read it and learned from it. Watt's argument that Defoe was the inventor of circumstantial detail in fiction will not hold up to close scrutiny.

By denying Defoe a patent on this technique, I do not mean to take away from his originality. In the 1690s, when Defoe developed as a writer, Locke and a number of other philosophers shifted the attention of writers like Defoe to the way in which reality is perceived—to the way in which objects appeared in the mind rather than to their existence as concrete realities. Watt first suggested that there was a relation between the new realism and the new epistemology, and I have tried to demonstrate its likelihood.[14] If this seems too intellectual for a writer like Defoe, it should be pointed out that Locke was quickly taken up by Presbyterian teachers and introduced into their academies.[15] He was regarded as an author to deal with even if one did not agree with his conclusions. Defoe was always lamenting the lack of concreteness in language and wishing for various methods of communicating more directly than words. If Defoe may indulge in an occasional catalogue of seemingly meaningless objects, he usually does it for a reason that goes beyond what appears in *The English Rogue*. He wishes to be concrete, but he also wishes to communicate something about the world that is perceived and the person perceiving. To be convinced of this, all one has to do is compare the scenes of the little boy losing his money in a tree that appear in *Colonel Jack* with Defoe's probable picaresque source, *The French Rogue* (1672). In the latter it is an amusing story. In Defoe's account, the event involves an overwhelming sense of loss that brings together a concrete sense of place and a real tree that is felt, reached into, walked about, and cried over. He didn't invent circumstantial realism, but he gave it a significance for fiction that it had never had before.

Watt's effort at establishing Defoe as a realist did little to raise his reputation in many modern critical circles, particularly those which prefer to believe that writers and artists imitate preexisting texts rather than nature. Pat Rogers, for example, has argued that to view Defoe, as Paul Hunter has contended, he should be examined, as a writer making continual allusions to biblical parables and tropes—as the creator of a type of allegory with a realistic surface—is to view him as a *better* writer than anyone had thought him to be.[16] Rogers finds discussions of Defoe's realism tedious. Indeed, the notion that Defoe was an allegorist has become so well established that modern critics often use this formulation without even bothering to argue the point. That it is a view which contravenes centuries of critical thought appears to disturb few.

For those critics who have always treated *realism* as a term applicable only to the nineteenth century and particularly to that part of the century that argued a doctrine of realism in the arts, the disappearance of Defoe as a claimant may be comforting,[17] but Defoe fulfills almost all the proclaimed ends of the realist movement.[18] He liked to depict the city in all its horror and ugliness. He was particularly interested in machines. Economic realities are never far away from his fictions. He preferred to treat characters among the middle or lower ranks of society. His descriptions were minute. He depicted common events such as picnics or outings. His novels focused on social problems—unemployment, poor street children, thieves and prostitutes, survival in the city. He defended his work as "sincere." Like later realists, Defoe, too, sought a language that would be direct and completely descriptive of the perceived object.

Although he was not a materialist and regarded the world of second causes, which he liked to describe in such detail, as governed by an all-knowing and all-powerful God, it would be hard to disqualify him on those grounds. There can be no conscious realism without a metaphysic, and whether that involves science or materialism or a traditional God does not reduce their contingency. In her excellent study of nineteenth-century art, *Realism*, Linda Nochlin points out the many myths and beliefs that underlay nineteenth-century realism—its belief in the nobility of labor, its tendency to depict scenes of evolution, its faith in science and the machine. She tries to distinguish between the realism of a Vermeer and that of a Manet, but her own lack of conviction is allowed to stand. No realism, she argues, can be an exact reflection of the external world. "This is a gross simplification," she writes, "for Realism was no more a mere mirror of reality than any other style, and its relation *qua* style to phenomenological data—the donnée—is as complex and difficult as that of Romanticism, the Baroque or Mannerism."[19]

It was Sir Walter Scott who first tried to explain the "general charm attached to the romances of De Foe," by referring it to "an appearance of REALITY to the incidents which he narrates."[20] He offers this solution after eliminating any possible virtues of style, language, plot, and story. Only recently have Defoe's stylistic virtues come under scrutiny. Scott's view that we read on because we believe we are experiencing something like life itself became the critical notion on which dozens of attacks and encomiums have been based. Certainly it is a judgment that at least takes into account one important element in Defoe's fiction. But the charm in Defoe's fiction has certain magical qualities as well. Realism was one element in a tendency to build convincing fictional worlds. Defoe's period was one that abandoned older myths and tried to shape new ones, and the concreteness of realistic fiction often gave flesh and blood to what might otherwise have been a highly abstract system of beliefs. The world of Defoe's fiction gives the impression of historic truth and reality. The underlying material often belongs to a world of abstract ideas, myth, and fantasy.

II

From Men we may descend to Action: and this prodigious Looseness of the Pen has confounded History and Fable from the beginning of both. Thus the great Flood in Deucalion's *Time is made to pass for the Universal Deluge: the Ingenuity of* Dedalus, *who by a Clue of Thread got out of the* Egyptian *Maze, which was thought impossible, is grown into a Fable of making himself a pair of Wings, and flying through the Air:—the great Drought and Violent Heat of Summer, thought to be the Time when the Great Famine was in* Samaria, *fabl'd by the Poets and Historians into the Story of* Phaeton *borrowing the Chariot of the Sun, and giving the Horses their Heads, they run so near the Earth as burnt up all the nearest Parts, and scorch'd the Inhabitants, so that they have been black in thos Parts ever since.*

These, and such like ridiculous Stuff, have been the Effects of the Pageantry of Historians in former Ages: and I might descend nearer home, to the Legends of Fabulous History which have swallow'd up the Actions of our ancient Predecessors, King Arthur, . . . *the Stories of* St. George *and the* Dragon, Guy Earl of Warwick, Bevis of Southampton, *and the like.* DEFOE, *The Storm*[21]

Discussions concerning the division between history and myth have furnished one of the more popular and productive exercises in contemporary thought. For Roland Barthes, myth represented a collection of established ideas used in a manner so as to produce stock responses. It is the picture of the black soldier in French uniform saluting the tricolor that in one sweep suggests the unity of France with its colonies and the fervor that colonial nations feel for their mother country. In short, it is a lie. History, on the contrary, is the naked truth insofar as truth can be determined. It avoids any means of communication, whether through language or picture, that would cause us to respond thoughtlessly.[22] For Lévi-Strauss, as for Mircea Eliade, myth is a far less noxious creation. It is the means by which a people succeed in moving themselves from a world of irreversible time into a synchronic world of ritual in which time is annihilated. As for history, Lévi-Strauss argues that it is partly illusory, an attempt to impose a partial organization of experience on the total flux of events. Meaning and direction have to be impressed on this flux to create history.[23]

This study of Defoe as a writer—his creative imagination, literary techniques, and realistic method—treats him as the inventor of mythical characters and situations in a real, historical environment. Recent critics have looked to biblical sources as the key to Defoe's tendency to give broad significance to his characters and their situations, but while such allusions are often meaningful, I would question whether the reader is always to be taken back into a total biblical context, whether the effect of Defoe's text is entirely typological. Such readings tend to ignore the self-contained quality of Defoe's narratives. In the sense that they innovate myths of their own—Robinson Crusoe, the isolated man; Colonel Jack, the self-made gentleman; Moll Flanders, the heroic female thief; Roxana, the quintessential courtesan—they force us forward rather than backward in time. It is as if his characters have subsumed all prior myths and make references to earlier models superfluous.

In this sense, Defoe's protagonists and their stories share the tendency toward self-contained systems in philosophy and law that developed during the late seventeenth century. It was common in such works to rejoice at creating a system that would function logically whether a God existed or not. The Boyle Lecturers, whose job it was to prove that God created and governed the universe, would deliberately avoid references to the Bible in working out their model theodicies. God's existence was wholeheartedly affirmed, of course, but his position was shifted from the base of all existence to the heavens where he acted as the overseer of a predominantly self-regulating system.

In creating their systems, writers like Thomas Hobbes, John Locke, Hugo Grotius, and Samuel Pufendorf had to rely on new kinds of myths and fictions about man, nature, and society, and their systems were essentially imaginative creations. Michael Oakeshott has remarked that "what makes *Leviathan* a masterpiece of philosophical literature is the profound logic of Hobbes' imagination, his power as an artist."[24] The history of the human mind that Sterne's Tristram perceives and admires so much in Locke's *Essay concerning Human Understanding* was viewed in negative terms by Locke's antagonist, Bishop Stillingfleet, who complained that Locke was merely spinning a systematic web out of his mind like a spider.[25] But both Stillingfleet and Sterne viewed Locke as the creator of a new myth of the self. And when Hume pointed out that the social contract as presented by Locke was merely a convenient fiction, he was hardly saying anything that would have surprised Locke himself. Locke was merely trying to present a generalized model for the development of government, and Hume rightly informs us that all such models are fictions.

A good example of the new type of reasonable myth for the development of human society appears at the beginning of Pufendorf's *History of Europe*. It was a passage that Defoe referred to approvingly in his own *Jure Divino*, a historical *"Satyr"* of epic length on political tyranny dedicated to the Goddess of Reason. Pufendorf starts out:

No man of Common Sense, imagines that at the first Propagation of Mankind, there were such Governments as are among us at this time. But in those Times each Father, without being Subject to any Superior Power, governed his Wife, Children and Servants, as a Sovereign. Nay, it seems very probable to me, that even to the time of the Deluge, there was no Magistracy or any Civil Constitution; but that the Government was lodged in each Father of his Family. For it is scarce to be imagined that such abominable Disorders could have been introduced, where the Power of Magistrates and Laws was exercised: And it is observable, that after once the Rules of Government were Constituted, we do not find that Mankind in general did run into the same Enormities, of which God Almighty was obliged to purge the World by an Universal Punishment, though the Root of the Evil was remaining as well after as before the Deluge. It seems also, that for a Considerable time after the Deluge this Paternal Government continued in the World.[26]

Compare this with the beginning of Raleigh's *History of the World:* "GOD, whom the wisest men acknowledg to be a Power uneffable, and Vertue infinite, a Light by abundant clarity invisible: and Understanding which it self can only comprehend, an Essence eternal and spiritual, of absolute pureness and simplicity; was, and is pleased to make himself known by the Work of the World."[27] What should be obvious from these beginnings is that something happened between the early seventeenth century and the latter part. In his history, Pufendorf is not really interested in theology. His prehistoric Europe is an anthropological model based on reason, the observations of primitive man by the explorers, and the Bible. The Bible is treated with respect as a historical account to argue for the universality of patriarchal government. Of course it is also the key to man's religious life, but Pufendorf's appeal is to common sense and reason.

As Leonard Krieger has argued, God is the capstone, not the basis, of Pufendorf's theories.[28] The same may be said for Hobbes and Locke. Such a change may seem small, but it would be a grave error to think that it did not have a pervasive effect. Vico might criticize Grotius for removing God as a necessary part of his system, yet he, too, created a new mythology—one based on a reinterpretation of ancient myths. And his God, like Pufendorf's, is given the comfortable position of being the guiding force of a system that operates fairly well without him. Not that any of these writers were atheists. To the contrary, with the possible exception of Hobbes, they were devout Christians, but they were reluctant to speculate too much about what was, in many ways, unknowable.

If not the most profound of thinkers, Defoe was perhaps the most versatile and prolific creator of systems in his age. In *Jure Divino* and the debates with Charles Leslie, he sketched out his political system, in works like *A Plan of the English Commerce* and *The Compleat English Tradesman* he developed his economic system, and from the very early *Essay upon Projects* to the very late *Protestant Monastery* he expatiated on his social schemes. In the latter work, he tried to show how a home for retired men and women might be made into a self-sufficient community. This concept informs various schemes that Defoe proposed in including a plan to settle the Palatine immigrants in undeveloped areas of Great Britain. It finds its way into his fiction in the communities established by those fleeing the plague in both *A Journal of the Plague Year* and *Due Preparations for the Plague*, in the common wealth of Libertalia founded by Defoe's pirate, Captain Missen, and in the island community founded by Robinson Crusoe and carried on by later settlers. In a sense, the very basis of Defoe's economic thinking may be found in a self-contained circular system of goods passing through many hands to establish a full circulation of trade through the nation.

When Defoe presented those systems as projects, they were accompanied by diagrams and statistics, all of which gave a sense of concreteness to his proposals. No wonder then, that when

George Bickham, THE WHIGS MEDLY *(1711). A caricature of Defoe appears at the top. The picture of Defoe placed between the Pope and the Devil is adapted from the Vandergucht portrait in Defoe's* JURE DIVINO *(1706).*

Defoe combined those social and political fictions with character and narrative, the effect was one of completeness. Ian Watt once argued that one ought not to extrapolate from Defoe's texts to events that are not there.[29] But the totality and circularity of Defoe's fictional worlds demand that we fill in gaps. If Moll Flanders says that she will not speak of her many adventures when she was in the Mint, are we not, given Defoe's presentation of a vivid environment and connections between events and objects, entitled to imagine events unrecorded? And no wonder that, for all their concreteness and individuality, his characters take on mythic proportions. On one level they are always mankind and womankind confronting situations as old as the human race.

Jure Divino is particularly significant in relation to Defoe's myth making because it was in this epic-length *"Satyr"* that Defoe sketched out his own historical and political myth. First he rid himself of the old Greco-Roman mythology and historiography by explaining the gods and goddesses away as mere human beings. This euhemerist explanation was common in Defoe's time, but few writers dismissed the past with such contempt as Defoe. The true history of mankind was the struggle against tyranny in the cause of liberty and property. The heroes of his epic were the monarchs who respected the laws and rights of their subjects. They were often heroes of the Protestant cause like Gustavus Adolphus and William III. But those members of the middle and lower ranks who fought for their rights and for the right of property were also heroes. Defoe was a firm believer in the inalienable right of self-defense and self-preservation, and he regarded such rights as equivalent to the rights of property. The archvillains were men like Louis XIV who appropriated the property of their own people as well as the lands of other nations. Only a few writers were more responsible for shaping and fashioning the Whig myth of history at the end of the seventeenth and beginning of the eighteenth century, but no one was as influential in disseminating that myth as Defoe.

Yet Defoe's great art lay in his ability to convey his myths as true history. Of course not everyone was convinced, but Defoe's tracts and treatises often have the same quality of vividness and conviction as his full-length fictions. And those fictions have the benefit of both realism and a powerful narrative interest. It was in those works that Defoe most fully achieved the power that he associated with true history. But if *Robinson Crusoe* can read as a treatise on economics, politics, theology, morality, and psychology, if Betteredge in Wilkie Collins's *The Moonstone* can practice Crusoemancy in the way that many Christians practiced bibliomancy, it is because Defoe was following the practices of his contemporaries in creating a systematic pattern of relationships. There is not much evidence that Betteredge is a man of deep religious faith, but he knows that the man without faith in Robinson Crusoe is worthless, *"a man with a screw loose in his understanding, or a man lost in the mist of his own self-conceit."*[30]

Betteredge does not read Robinson Crusoe as allegory; he reads it as the truth. And that element of factual and psychological truth in Defoe's fiction owes much to its basis in history. Although some writers before Defoe had voiced doubts about the possibility of a truly accurate history, most believed that history could serve as a verifiable, correct record of the past. And few doubted that a knowledge of the past was a key to the present. One of Defoe's favorite words of contempt for the argument of an opponent was *chimera*, which was equivalent to *myth* in the sense of something without reasonable or historical content, and one of the marks of his writing is a tendency to appeal to history and its lessons. Critics have too often searched for puritan moral bookkeeping or middle-class taste to explain the factuality of Defoe's fiction, when the proper model of imitation may simply have been the factual records of history and life itself.

But there is little that is purely rational about either Defoe's politics or his fictions, and a recent critic has suggested that we might as well ignore that dedication to the Goddess of Reason before *Jure Divino*.[31] True enough, when he praised himself for his wonderful "Mythological manner," in one of his journals, he must have realized that the phrase had overtones that went beyond complimenting himself for his ability to handle narrative.[32] And one would have to admit that when Dr. Joseph Browne suggested that Defoe's voyage to the moon, *The Consolidator*, and other writings revealed a wild and uncontrolled imagination, there was some truth to the charge.[33]

The consequence was a fiction rooted in reality and history but with the generality of myth and fairy tale, a fiction which, to use

Coleridge's words, reconciles "the general with the concrete; the idea with the image; the individual, with the representative."[34] As a result, Defoe's characters are both highly individualized and mythic, firmly based in history, and capable of floating free from time. Robinson Crusoe may serve as economic man, political man, and religious man, as man the voyager, man the day-dreamer, and man the master of his environment. Moll Flanders, who had many of the qualities of the historical figure, Moll King, quickly assumed a life of her own as a master criminal and master survivor, living on in chapbooks that Defoe would scarcely have recognized as a remnant of his own creation. Yet she is still there as the mythic woman, enduring all kinds of adversity, managing to survive husbands and lovers, both bad and good, an indifferent economic order, and her own destructive urge to marry a gentleman. And Roxana, with a personal style all her own, becomes *the* Fortunate Mistress. Defoe has seldom been given proper credit for creating or at least reshaping the myths on which so many novels have been based.[35]

III

But Sir, their needs no other Proof of his binomical Performance, than the agreeableness of the stile and manner; the little Art he is truly Master of, of forging a Story and imposing it on the World for Truth. WEEKLY JOURNAL, *November 1718*

. . . and this was the Method of the great Men in the East, in the Ages of Hieroglyphicks, when Things were more accurately Describ'd by Emblems and Figures than Words; and even our Saviour himself took this Method of Introducing the Knowledge of himself into the World, (viz.) By Parables and Similitudes. DEFOE, *Review*[36]

The writer of the letter to J. Read's *Weekly Journal* thought that he was conceding little to Daniel Defoe in granting him that "little Art" of telling stories. He proceeds to illustrate his argument against Defoe by demonstrating how a recent account of a murder from Defoe's pen was filled with "all the little Embellishments of Lies" that made it appear vivid and authentic. "I remember my Grandmother us'd to tell a Story like this," he sneered, "and I wish the Author of the *White-Hall Post* was not acquainted with the old Gentlewoman, or that his own Grandmother, was not as great a Liar as mine." This writer associated storytelling with garrulous old women, and in this notion of prose narratives he was not alone.[37] But for better or for worse, the story was equivalent to Defoe's "Hieroglyphicks." He regarded the brief narrative example as the most direct way of communicating his ideas.[38]

Many of Defoe's critics have stressed the oddity of his sudden emergence as a writer of fiction in 1719 with the publication of *Robinson Crusoe*, and in a recent work devoted to Defoe's social and economic thought, Peter Earle confesses that he cannot explain Defoe's fictions at all.[39] But the writer of the letter to the *Weekly Journal* in 1718 regarded the "forging a Story" the real mark of Defoe's work. All of this suggests that his contemporaries knew Defoe much better than many modern critics. Narrative was always Defoe's real talent, whether the short anecdote in a prose tract or an imaginary voyage like *The Consolidator*. And with the discovery of the manuscript "Historical Collections" of 1682, I can say with certainty, in the beginning was the story.

The second work listed in John Robert Moore's *A Checklist of the Writings of Daniel Defoe*[40] is a manuscript whose existence was first reported by Walter Wilson in his life of Daniel Defoe. Wilson noted that a dissenting minister, John Duncan, in a history of his church at Winborne, had written: "I am in possession of two manuscript volumes of Daniel De Foe's. One is corrected for the press, with a dedication. He wrote a neat fair hand. He entitles the book thus: Historical Collections: or, Memoirs of Passages collected from several Authors, 1682. I think it would take well if it were published. I have also some original poems of his, in his own handwriting."[41] The title is quoted correctly except it should be "Passages & stories." Wilson stated that he was unable to discover the volumes. The poems, Defoe's *Meditations*, came to light in a Huntington Library manuscript, but the "Historical Collections" were only a name to Moore as they had been to Wilson. Moore speculated that they might be a list of parallel dates such as appears at the end of *Memoirs of a Cavalier*. But "Historical Collections," which I recently discovered at the William Andrews Clark Memorial Library, is actually a series of little histories or "apophthegmes" that Defoe, under the sobriquet of Bellmour, collected for his Clarinda as a present of his affection.

In his dedication to Clarinda, Defoe said that he was not going to change the style or subject matter of his sources. They were to be a gift of his "Juvenal Readings," little stories that would entertain and tell the truth about life. In fact, Defoe always changed the stories, and the ways in which he revised them as well as the selections themselves are a clue to his early thinking and daydreams. Take, for example, a simple story drawn from Plutarch, a story illustrating success through patience:

Popilius held out a long time against the whole power of the Romans; at last Marius was sent against him who perceiving himself to weake to Encounter with him Placed himself on the tope of a Hill, lingring there because of his weakness, which Siloe perceiving, Defyeing him said If thou art a man of thy hands and has any heart O Marius come downe and fight with me Nay (answered Marius) But if thou art such a fellowe as thou art accounted to be compell me by force to Come Downe or else waite my leisure.[42]

The version in North's translation of Plutarch is: "It is said also that *Popedius Silo.* who was the chiefest Captaine of reputation and Authority the Enemies had, said unto *Marius* one a time. If thou be Marius, so great a Captaine as they say thou art, leave thy Campe and come out to Battell. Nay, said *Marius* to him againe: If thou be a great Captaine, pluck me out by the Eares, and compell me to come to Battell."[43] I give this simply as an example of the kinds of changes that Defoe made in retelling his story. Defoe tends to change it from an anecdote with a particular verbal flavor ("pluck me out by the Eares") to a narrative with a location, a cause for Marius's reaction ("his weakness"), and a response which carries a certain dignity that Defoe wishes to give to the character of Marius.

The changes illustrate the transformation from the jest books of the seventeenth century to a new type of narrative—a narrative that expanded the possibilities of character and motivation.[44] Whether in a brief story like this or in a historical account, such changes amounted to the addition of fictional material and interpretation. Sections of Plutarch similar to this passage were often included in collections of anecdotes. Defoe, in a marginal note, refers at one point to Nicholas Udall's translations of the *Apophthegmes* of Erasmus. But Defoe is not interested in the kind of quick turn to be found in most of Erasmus's examples; he is interested in the potential insight that they provide for understanding human nature. For example, he tells a story that he will later use in his *Memoirs of Cavalier*. It concerns a commander who, to encourage his troops, tells them they may keep whatever they find in the process of sacking a city. A common soldier discovers the city mint with its considerable amount of money. The commander holds to his word and allows the soldier to keep his wealth. Defoe adds a comment to this: "A rare example of abstinence."[45] In his later novel, George, the servant of the Cavalier, recovers a great deal of wealth on the battlefield. The Cavalier allows him to keep it and treats George as a "Gentleman" from that time forward.[46] What interested Defoe was the situation as it involved the characters of the commander and the common soldier. The brief anecdote contained in it a world (one might say a novel) of possibilities for Defoe.

Another example of a particular account that left an indelible impression on Defoe was one that became the basis for many of his fictions—the account of the person who is haunted by a crime committed in the past and who is eventually destroyed by the secret gnawing at his conscience:

A Man haveing killed another willfully in London, to avoid the stroak of Justice fled beyond the seas, where he lived fifteen yeares without any Discovery. At last he resolved to Returne, But the horrour of his Conscience so terrefyed him as soon as he Descried the English shore that he was almost frantick and beeing arrived he landed at Queen-Hithe as soone as he coame on shore he fell a Running as fast as if for life no man persueing him. At last he fell Downe, at or neare the same place where he had Done the murther. And Immediately cryed out, It was I, It was I did it. Being asked what he had done; he answered It was I killed the man; The people told him he was distracted, he answered the third time I say it was I killed the man: they carryed him before a Justice, where he still answered as before, and search being then made it was found that he had indeed killed the man fifteen yeares of late, for which Divine vengance had p'sued him and justily overtaken him & he was then deservedly Executed.[47]

Defoe told this story many times with many variations, and the end of *Roxana* is based partly on this theme.[48] As we shall see, it became a major idea in the English novel carrying with it the irony of either a conscience that cannot be appeased or of a past life that will not be put aside.

The selection of little "histories" in "Historical Collections" reveals that Defoe was attracted to stories that illustrated the presence of Providence, to tales of poor men and women who somehow succeeded in life through some stroke of fortune, to tales of heroes like Alexander and Scanderberg, and to almost anything having to do with the Turks and their wars against Christendom. They tell us much about his fascination with narrative and show that from the very beginning he was able to evoke a sense of wonder in combination with a feeling for the right kind of detail. But they also remind us that Defoe wanted his stories to have significance and that he wanted that significance to emerge from the narrative without any direct commentary. The marginal note that I quoted above is a rare example. The writer who applauded his own ingenuity in composing, without any direct reference to contemporary events, a fable about the split among the Whigs that resulted in Walpole's withdrawal from the government was the same Daniel Defoe who wanted the narratives of "Historical Collections" to communicate their meanings directly and without any explanation.[49] At least the potential powers of a novelist were present in 1682.

In beginning this work with discussions of realism, the process of incorporating mythic significance in his narratives and its odd combination with historical truth, and the essential attraction of narrative itself, I have selected only a few essential ingredients for Defoe's fiction. In the sections that follow, I attempt to explore other aspects of Defoe's work, from the real events that occurred in the England of his time that inspired the fictions and fantasies of *Robinson Crusoe* to the ways in which Defoe created many of the myths that went into the Newgate Calendar and the novels drawn from that work. I have not attempted to touch systematically on all of Defoe's narratives. Rather, I have aimed at examining certain creative processes that explain why, after all these years, Defoe is still considered a great writer.

2
Imaginary Islands and Real Beasts:
The Imaginative Genesis of *Robinson Crusoe*

He [Defoe] is always raising Apparitions in the Air, Encountering Fantastick Daemons in his Imagination, or Fighting with his own Shadow . . . . I fancy he keeps a Correspondence still with the Moon, *or at least delights in strange monsterous Stories, Things that are not familiarly known or believed, but out of the common way of vulgar Thinking.* JOSEPH BROWNE, *A Dialogue between Church and No-Church; or, A Rehearsal of the Review*[1]

. . . nor is it possible to describe how many various Shapes affrighted Imagination represented Things to me in, how many wild Ideas were found every Moment in my Fancy, and what strange unaccountable Whimsies came into my thoughts by the Way. DANIEL DEFOE, *The Life and Strange Surprising Adventures of Robinson Crusoe*[2]

MOST RECENT studies of *Robinson Crusoe* have tried to fix its meaning and to assign it to the traditions, whether fictional, spiritual, or intellectual, to which it belongs. Without in any way disparaging these efforts, to which I have contributed my share, I want to change direction and, in the following pages, trace the workings of Defoe's mind in the years preceding the publication of *Robinson Crusoe* on 25 April 1719 to discover what may have moved his imagination. I am not particularly interested in sources. Doubtless his mind was profoundly stirred by the experiences of a number of castaways—Alexander Selkirk's on Juan Fernandez, Robert Knox's in Ceylon, and Robert Drury's on Madagascar.[3] But Defoe was a writer whose "mythological Manner," as he called his ability to shape a fiction, was stirred by contemporary events.[4] Finding accounts of piracy or theft that triggered the composition of *Captain Singleton* or *Moll Flanders* is not a major problem. *Robinson Crusoe,* however, seems to be different. It shares with James Thomson's *The Seasons,* a work of roughly the same period, a concern for large and sublime themes—isolation, storms, floods, shipwrecks.

What I want to show is that *Crusoe* is in many ways the product of certain contemporary events, and that Defoe's imagination was particularly stirred toward a depiction of the terrible and the sublime. I want to locate Crusoe's island in Defoe's mind as he conceived it. Gaston Bachelard says in *The Poetics of Space,* "Memories are motionless, and the more securely they are fixed in space, the sounder they are. To localize a memory in Time is merely a matter for the biographer and only corresponds to a sort of external history, for external use, to be communication to others . . . . For a knowledge of intimacy, localization in the spaces of our intimacy is more urgent than determination of dates."[5] Although I will give dates to suggest the immediacy of some of Defoe's thoughts, I will be concerned mainly with the way certain events become images and with the process of "autovalorization," to use Bachelard's term, by which for Defoe and Crusoe the cave becomes a house and then a castle, and his stay on the island his reign rather than his captivity.

I

After Defoe's death, the *Grub-Street Journal* printed an account of his arrival in the Elysian Fields:

As to poets, we are prodigiously overstocked with them . . . that universal genius, Mr. D——F——e lately arrived raises our admiration here as much as he did yours when alive. Among other things he frequently entertains us with accounts of the various ways of diverting the living world with newspapers, an amusement altogether unknown in the age of Augustus. He assures us that he himself at one and the same time wrote two celebrated papers, one on the Whig and one on the Tory side, with which each party were extremely well pleased.[6]

Indeed, during the years before *Robinson Crusoe* appeared, Defoe became a journalist in a way that he had not been previously. His early newspapers, the *Review* and *Mercator,* were actually essays on one or more aspect of current events. He might discuss trade or the affairs of Scotland for months at a time. Whereas most other papers printed news items from home and abroad, Defoe avoided such a practice and even noted with some pride that he had once refused a job as a translator of foreign news.[7] But after 1716 he was deep into reporting the events of daily life. In *Mercurius Politicus* (1716–20) and *Mercurius Britannicus* (1718–19), he put together the news in a monthly digest, and in the *Weekly Journal* (1717–24) and the *White-Hall Evening Post* (1718–20) he treated the news in more detail. As the *Grub-Street Journal* states, and as enemies like J. Read and Abel Boyer suggested at the time, Defoe's journalistic ventures involved him in writing for both Whig and Tory, but we should not be surprised if both sides "were extremely well pleased."[8] Factional newspapers are useless if no one reads them, and Defoe, like Norman Mailer today, had the power of entertaining his readers. It was he, not Nathaniel Mist, the publisher of the *Weekly Journal*, who described himself as "an odd sort of a Fellow inclin'd now and then to a little humerous Mirth."[9]

All of this is well known, but no writer on Defoe has discussed the effect that this plunge into writing and editing day-by-day events had on his mind and art. In his biography of Defoe, John Robert Moore separated his careers as journalist and novelist into different facets of his life, but the particular kind of journalism he undertook around 1716 exactly parallels the start of his writing memoirs, moral dialogues, and fiction.

Much of Defoe's journalism during those years has been put into two volumes edited by William Lee in 1869.[10] Some of Lee's items have been regarded with suspicion, and indeed he included some seemingly neutral news items that could be found in almost the same form in any of five newspapers published at that time. A careful reading of these papers side by side, however, reveals how crucial that *almost* can be. At times an adjective is added to suggest political overtones; often a few words will make the difference between factual reporting and an attack on the government. To discover exactly where accounts of piracy or theft in the pages of *Mercurius Politicus* or the *Weekly Journal* reflected on James Stanhope or other Whig office holders might be impossible for the modern reader, but apparently such innuendoes did not escape contemporary readers. And if they failed to catch the parallel, occasional denials of such intentions would underscore it for the dullest reader. Defoe may not have written a few items in Lee's collection, but he certainly read carefully those pieces he did not write or edit. His fiction reveals the extent to which those labors moved his imagination.

Some of those items had a simple and direct influence on his writing. For example, in the *Weekly Journal* of 7 February 1719, he announced a new scheme for a colony at the mouth of the Orinoco where Crusoe was to be shipwrecked:

We expect, in two or three Days, a most flaming Proposal from the South Sea Company, or from a Body of Merchants who claim kindred of them, for erecting a British Colony on the Foundation of the South-Sea Company's Charter, upon the Terra Firma, or the Northermost Side of the Mouth of the great River Oroonoko. They propose, as we hear, the establishing a Factory and Settlement there, which shall cost the Company 500000£. Sterling, and they demand the Government to furnish six Men of War, and 4000 regular Troups, with some Engineers and 100 Pieces of Cannon, and military Stores in Proportion for the maintaining and supporting the Design; for which they suggest, that the Revenue it shall bring to the Kingdom will be a full amends. It is said they will send over Workmen to build 12 Sloops with 12 Guns each, and able to carry 300 Men, which are to maintain a Commerce up the Great River to the Province or Empire of Guiana, in which they resolve to establish a new Colony also, above 400 Leagues from the first Settlement, to be always supplied with Forces as well as Merchandizes from the first Settlement; and they doubt not to carry on a Trade there equal to that of the Portuguese in the Brazils, and to bring home an equal quantity of Gold, as well as to cause a prodigious Consumption of our British Manufactures. This, it seems, is the same Country and River discovered by Sir Walter Rawleigh, in former Days, and that which he miscarried in by several Mistakes, which may now easily be prevented.[11]

Such a report suggests that I was correct in arguing some time ago that *Robinson Crusoe* took its rise from Defoe's activities as a propagandist for colonization. The title of the second part of the novel was often changed in later editions to stress this point, and were one to speculate on the contemporary report that set everything in motion, this would be the likeliest place to begin.[12]

But I am less interested here in theories of colonization than in the way the daydream of a colony filled his mind with thoughts of Sir Walter Raleigh and how that imagined colony became Defoe's and Crusoe's island. "In the family sitting-room," Bachelard remarks, "a dreamer of refuges dreams of a hut, or a nest, or of nooks and corners in which he would like to hide away like an animal in his hole."[13] Crusoe's island colony must have been the product of one of Defoe's oldest daydreams. He turned it into great art by extending his own dream of an island cave into Crusoe's imaginative daydream of castles and kingdoms. But we must start with the island colony, for here was the place where he could transform the materials of newspapers and pamphlets into the magic of fiction. Here he could transmute contemporary arguments over the shortages of silver coins and the poor quality of copper coins into Crusoe's famous speech on the uselessness of gold on an island without a need for exchange and not much real need for labor.[14] And the rather strange announcement in the *Weekly Journal* on 19 April 1718 of a scheme to raise all kings to the status of emperors and all men with full political control of an area to the rank of king could be made to work on Crusoe's island even if it never came to fruition in Europe. For Defoe, the island was a place like Marianne Moore's poetic garden—an island of imaginary trees with real toads in them.

II

Of major economic and theological significance throughout the novel is Crusoe's belief that his refusal to obey the wishes of his father that he follow the even life of the middle class is the reason that God punishes him, first with slavery and then with isolation. And it may suggest considerable personal involvement in Crusoe's story, for Defoe was a father whose last years were embittered by a disobedient son.[15] But if the first volume of *The Family Instructor* (1715) shows the terrible death of an atheistic son who outrages his kind father, the second volume (1718) ends with an exemplary story of a passionate father who almost murders one of his own sons. After agreeing to surrender his business to his children, he accuses them of plotting against him and reassumes control of his affairs, only to relinquish it once more when his irrepressible passions provoke him to a near-murderous outburst against one of his workmen. The conflict between fathers and sons, then, was hardly a new theme for Defoe, and one of his last pieces, *Chickens Feed Capons* (1730), a revision of his *The Protestant Monastery* (1726), returns to it with such vehemence that one cannot help but think he has been reading *King Lear*.

In fact, during 1718 this family conflict was acted out on the level of kings and princes. In England the Prince of Wales and King George I began to find each other's company unbearable, and the prince moved away from court. This was an event Defoe considered too dangerous to write about directly, leaving it to future historians "when our Posterity shall speak with an unrestrained Liberty."[16] Meanwhile, in Russia, Peter the Great accused his son Alexei of criminal disobedience. Here there could be no need for censorship, and as Defoe followed this story in *Mercurius Politicus* and the *Weekly Journal*, it became increasingly terrifying. At first Alexei was accused of leaving the country without seeking permission of his father. The czar announced that he had confessed his guilt,

> but alledging the Weakness of his Parts and Genius, which did not permit him to apply himself to Sciences and other Functions recommended to him, he acknowledged himself incapable and unworthy of our Succession, desiring us to discharge him of the same . . . . But forgetting the Fear and Commandment of God, who enjoyns Obedience even to Private Parents, and much more to those who are at the same time Sovereigns, Our Cares had no other return than an unheard of ingratitude from him.[17]

Peter then stated that Alexei had put himself under his "Protection" after renouncing his right to the throne.

After relating these events, Defoe commented briefly that he believed "no History can equal it, and perhaps never may." But when the czar began punishing some of his nobility who did not approve his actions, even going so far as to use the *"Potoque,"* which involved stripping one Russian lady naked and administering four hundred lashes, Defoe exclaimed "Monstrum Horrendum."[18] And when Alexei appeared to have been apprehended for complicity in a plot to assassinate his father, Defoe began to draw analogies to the situation in England on both the royal and private level:

Who could honestly stand up for such a Father, or pity such a Son, where Irreconcileableness and Stubborness meet? Where the Father embraces all the Opportunities he can find to distress the Son, who in return not only repels his Efforts, but labours to ruin his interest by disturbing his Measures? Can anyone imagine that he can love any Person that hates his own Son? Or that such a Son can esteem, obey, honour, reverence, or be grateful to anything Human or Divine that can dash Nature out of his Constitution?[19]

The Tory point of view tended to defend the son against the father and, by implication, the Prince of Wales against George I. But when Alexei died "for fear of Death, *as a certain writer used to call it,*" that is, fear that his father might execute him, Defoe loses some of his sympathy for him, even in his Tory papers.[20]

At the same time that these events were occurring, Defoe was following a more domestic story of disobedience involving a Quaker potter named William Oades and his sons. The sons apparently schemed to have their father arrested in an effort to assume control of the family business. Then, according to reports in the *Weekly Journal,* they fired a gun from the window of their home in an effort to kill their mother but hit a stranger instead. The father, instead of taking revenge, actually attempted to free his sons after they had been arrested.[21] Defoe might have thought all of this good human interest material, but his involvement was far from detached.

All of these stories had different endings. There was, of course, no way of patching up the quarrel in Russia, and George I might have envied Peter his good luck. The Prince of Wales remained alive to annoy him throughout his life. Oades succeeded in getting his sons freed in spite of rumors that they would be transported. In the 1715 *Family Instructor,* the prodigal son dies unrepentant and raving before his father can arrive, and in the second volume the passionate father comes to terms with his sons even if he can never master his passionate anger. As for Crusoe, for all his suffering, he finds an island kingdom that he half believes provides him with greater contentment than he ever met in his former life. And he also finds that he feels real happiness only when he is close to his "Castle," which has an odd resemblance to the very tradesman's shop his father might have wanted for him.[22]

Frontispiece to the first English edition of ROBINSON CRUSOE *(1719).*

III

There are, of course, numerous storms in *Robinson Crusoe*, the most vivid one being that which carries Crusoe to his island and which pursues him to the land with one wave "as high as a great Hill, and as furious as an Enemy" (p. 44). One may see in these storms a spiritual metaphor, though even in Crusoe's narrative, the terror induced by nature in storm is more the potential occasion for turning man's mind toward death and the terrors of an afterlife without a share in Christian salvation than a direct act of God's wrath. And Defoe's fascination with violent tempests, like his interest in plagues, lies deeper than his conscious search after that God whom he knew to be the first cause of such events.[23] His book on the great storm of 1703 is a detailed account of a terrifying and sublime event. All disasters, floods, fires, earthquakes, famines, war, as well as storms and plagues moved him profoundly. Like many painters of the second half of the eighteenth century (one thinks immediately of Loutherbourg and early Turner) and the Gothic novelists, Defoe was intrigued by human distress in the face of natural disasters.[24] He was particularly proud of his rendering of thirst and starvation in the second part of *Robinson Crusoe,* a scene that he foreshadows in the first volume when Crusoe contemplates his fate while the current is carrying his little boat away from his island. The account of the starving widow and her child as told by their maid has something of the quality of Géricault's *Raft of the Medusa:*

I fell into a violent Passion of Crying, and after that had a second Fit of violent Hunger; I got up ravenous, and in a most dreadful condition; had my Mistress been dead, as much as I lov'd her, I am certain I should have eaten a Piece of her Flesh, with as much Relish, and as unconcern'd, as ever I did the Flesh of any Creature appointed for Food; and once or twice I was going to bite into my own Arm: At last, I saw the Bason in which was the Blood I had bled at my Nose the Day before; I ran to it and swallow'd it with much Haste, and such a greedy Appetite, as if I had wonder'd no Body had taken it before. [III, 67]

The ship she was on was the victim of a hurricane, a second storm, and then a "strong Gale of Wind" (II, 135). From the very beginning, then, the storm and its effects lie at the very heart of *Robinson Crusoe* and contribute to the sublime mood Defoe wanted to evoke.

Given our knowledge of Defoe's interests, then, it is not surprising that his weekly and monthly journals are taken up with accounts of storms, and more particularly with one storm that struck northern Europe around Christmas 1717. Defoe's mind went back to the storm of 1703 in drawing comparisons, and after estimating the death toll on human life at somewhere between forty and a hundred thousand, he remarked, "In a Word, the Dreadfulness of this Calamity is not to be express'd; no Eye can bear the Sight of the Misery of the Country without Tears, nor any Ear can hear the Distress of the poor wretches Remains that are left without the utmost horror." He described how the survivors were in "the utmost Terror and Amazement." Many in Holland fled to the fortress of Delzyle, which was in turn threatened with destruction, "the Water having risen above the Top of the Bastion of the Fortifications, and the People remaining in the uppermost Rooms of their Houses, expecting Death every Hour." In the midst of the swollen waters could be seen "floating, innumerable dead Bodies, Cattle, Roofs of Houses, and Household Stuff."[25]

A ship from Hamburg found a family of seven clinging to one of these roofs: "the poor Creatures were in the utmost Distress, and the poor Children almost perish'd with Cold." The force of the storm drove a number of ships onto the shore, including an English ship; the captain and forty-four men survived while one hundred and fifty drowned. Not only was Defoe interested in these accounts, but he knew that writing about them was one of his talents. He printed a letter from a J. S. in one of his journals congratulating him on "the best and most distinct Account of the Storm and Innundation in Holland, etc. of any Writer whatever."[26]

Although that storm inspired Defoe's most vivid descriptions in the years preceding the publication of *Robinson Crusoe,* he also maintained a running account of the various sea fights between England and Spain, between the Turks and Venetians, and between the Sallee pirates and any ship unfortunate enough to fall in their way. Crusoe, of course, is captured by the Sallee rovers on his first independent voyage to the coast of Guinea, and in this he was hardly alone. In an incident reported by one of Defoe's newspapers a John Armstrong was reported as the only survivor of a sea fight with the Moors. Rescued by his enemies, he was taken to join five hundred other English prisoners.[27] Although Professor Starr has accurately described accounts of Barbary as a "seventeenth-century Genre,"[28] there must have been enough interest in those events for Mist to advertise at that time a novel called *Zulima*, which rehearsed the familiar theme of the love between a noble slave and a Moorish princess.[29] Crusoe meets no beautiful Moorish princess, but his account of slavery in Sallee is vivid enough. As for Defoe's newspapers, when a treaty was arranged between England and the rovers, they shifted to other sea wrecks, fights, and storms.

On 20 September 1718, he printed an account in the *Weekly Journal* of the wreck of a ship belonging to the Venetian fleet:

They were surpriz'd with a terrible Tempest which entirely dispers'd the entire Fleet, the greatest Part of them being driven on Shoar among the Rocks on the Coast of Epirus, where they are dash'd in pieces by the Violence of the Sea, and very few of the People sav'd; that of eight men of War they have not heard but of one; that five of the Gallies are stranded on that Island; that most of the Transports have run the same Fate; that what was still an Addition to their Misery, many of those that escaped the Sea have been massacred by the Mountaineers; that the brave General Schulemberg, got on Shore with great Difficulty, the Man of War which he was in being brake to pieces; but that he had much also to defend himself against the Country People afterwards and some say still that he is killed.

And nearer home he reported the damage caused by a dramatic high tide in the Thames. Again, in *Mercurius Politicus*, he told of an accident in the Thames. A boat with eighteen passengers coming from Gravesend was overturned by a sudden gust of wind, and "no less than Seventeen of the Eighteen were Drown'd, none escaping but a little Boy, who with great Difficulty swam on Shore."[30]

The year 1718 was one of extraordinary happenings at sea, from reports of the effects of the flood at the beginning of the year to the victory of Admiral George Byng over the Spanish fleet at Cape Passaro. One event must have inspired the idea of starvation at sea referred to before. On 7 June 1718, Defoe gave an account of a ship driven by storms to the South Seas where, "falling short of Provisions, and there being 200 Men on board, they were all starved to Death but the Captain and five others, who after they made Land, came ashoar and all died."[31] Crusoe was more like Schulemberg. He survived, and though at the beginning he did not have to fight the people of the country, he did eventually have to confront the "wild Beasts or Men" (p. 71) of his fears.

IV

When Crusoe comes to cast up his account of the good and bad of his condition, he balances the comparative peacefulness of his island against other possibilities:

I am without any Defence. or Means to resist any Violence of Man or Beast. But I am cast on an Island where I see no wild Beasts to hurt me, as I saw on the Coast of Africa: And what if I had been Shipwreck'd there? [P. 66]

Though Crusoe is eventually threatened by the arrival of cannibals on his island, these would seem to be part of a general fear that he has from the beginning of being devoured by beasts. Within approximately thirty pages of his landing on the island the possibility of confronting wild beasts is mentioned some eleven times.

When Crusoe escapes from Sallee with Xury and sails along the coast of Africa, he describes the beasts that appear at the spring to drink: "We heard such dreadful Noises of the Barking, Roaring, and Howling of Wild Creatures, of we knew not what Kinds, that the poor Boy was ready to die with Fear" (p. 24). Crusoe confesses his ignorance of what the "mighty Creatures" that come swimming out to the boat could be, and though Xury identifies them as lions, all Crusoe is aware of is "hideous Howlings and Yellings" (p. 25) and the "hideous Cryes and Howlings" (p. 25) raised by the animals after he fires his gun. Crusoe reports Xury's fears but says little about his own reaction. Some days later, however, he wounds a lion and gives Xury the courage to take a gun and kill the animal by putting the muzzle close to his ear, an action which Friday later repeats in a snowy landscape when he and Crusoe are crossing the Pyrenees.

These repetitions, including the second shooting of an animal in the water, have a dreamlike quality, and if E. M. Tillyard is right in suggesting that this recurrent motif helps to organize the work and to prefigure what is to come, there is nevertheless something of the feeling of the repeated nightmare.[32] In the beginning, at least, the terror is undercut by certain comic elements. Thus, in his confrontation with the dying goat in the cave that he discovers, there are certain elements of farce in the account of how his fears of having encountered the devil caused his hair to stand on end enough to lift his cap off his head. It ends with his imagining himself "like one of those ancient Giants, which are said to live in Caves, and Holes, in the Rocks, where none could come at them" (p. 179). Crusoe is not so terrified at the prospect of the cannibals at this point that he cannot imagine himself larger than life, a primitive cave dweller battling wild beasts and men or, once he finds the cave a grotto encrusted with "precious Stones, or Gold" (p. 179), a visionary such as Poll's name for him, "Poor Robin," suggests.[33]

Much of this dwelling on beasts arises from two nightmarish reports that Defoe printed in the *Weekly Journal* of 8 March 1718 about a floating island filled with beasts and about towns in the Pyrenees invaded by hungry beasts of all kinds. The sailors who encountered the floating island "heard hideous Noises in it of the Roaring of wild ravenous Beasts, such as Lions, Panthers, Tygers, Wolves, and the like, who make a most horrible and frightful Roaring and Howling." Defoe theorized that the island must have broken away from a larger body of land after an earthquake, but he could not explain how it might float. He was more detailed on the events in the Pyrenees: "Another thing remarkable from abroad, is concerning an Irruption of the most hideous Armies of wild and furious Beasts, from the Mountains of the Pyranese, who being starved out of their Dens, by the unusual Depth and Continuance of the Snow and Cold came down as well on the Spanish Side, into the Low Lands of Aragon and Catalonia, as on the French Side into the Plains and Forrests of Roussilon and Languedoc." The "Armies" were composed of bears, wolves, and lynxes. In one town they tore apart two men, but a "third having more Courage, stood his Ground; and one of the Bears rising upon him, he clapt his piece into his Mouth, and shot him dead on the Spot." After the townspeople succeeded in driving the animals from this town, much like the beasts on the floating island, they "set up the most hideous Cries that ever was heard, which was answer'd again by a confus'd Noise of Roarings and Howling from a farther Distance, that several People in the village were frightened to Death, and never recover'd."

This is of course the scene for the battle with the wolves on the way through the Pyrenees to France, though the comedy in Friday's shooting the bear seems a far cry from the townsman who shoots the bear in the mouth. Defoe took his military image much farther in *Robinson Crusoe* where the wolves attack "most of them in a Line, as regularly as an Army drawn up by experienc'd Officers" (III, 97). But then the incident echoes the attack made on the cannibals, just as the scene of the bodies of two men nearly devoured by the wolves seems to repeat the bloody scene at the remains of the cannibals' feast. Of course Crusoe's account of the defense against the wolves is made in terms imagined but never realized in his thoughts of the attacks of the cannibals. The wolves make a "furious Charge" against Crusoe's "Breast Work" (III, 99) like an army attacking a fortification, and in this charge there is a strange resemblance to the accounts of the wars in Italy and around Belgrade.[34] But I do not want to carry parallels too far. To suggest that Defoe's imagination was possessed with scenes of human and animal slaughter when he came to write *Robinson Crusoe* should be sufficient for my purpose.

V

No one can doubt that the story of Alexander Selkirk's lonely years on Juan Fernandez impressed Defoe, but given his tendency to merge single events into an archetypal narrative, it would be surprising if, in his imagination, Selkirk's experience did not blend with an entire tradition of isolates. An examination of his journalism again reveals that there occurred in April 1718 a trial of three men who had revolted against Captain Randal of the ship *Anglesey*, "in which they were Sailors, and forced him to go on Shore, with his Mate and Boatswain in an uninhabited island in *America*, without any thing for their Subsistance, or without Arms for their Defence, where they must in all Probability Perish for want of Food, or be Devour'd for want of Arms to defend themselves; in this Condition they left them and run away with the Ship, after which they turn'd Pirates: But they were taken by a *French* Man of War and surrendered to Justice."[35] In addition to this incident, which bears an obvious relationship to the events leading to Crusoe's rescue at the end, Defoe reported numerous maroonings and wrecks, including that of a Spanish ship commanded by the Marquess Mari which allowed the crew, like Crusoe, sufficient time to "plunder the Ship."[36]

But critics who have found symbolic significance in Crusoe's island and his exile have undoubtedly been correct. The daydream voyage to an imaginary island, like the fictional genre of the imaginary voyage, may involve considerable realistic detail, but it is still a device for getting the reader to the place where an adventure will occur or where a utopian scheme will be unveiled. When Defoe claimed that his work was "Allegorical," we may certainly agree if we accept Angus Fletcher's notion of allegory, and when Defoe suggested it was autobiographical ("Historical"), we may accept this too, if we conceive of literature in broadly phenomenological terms.[37] Thus, even Defoe's discussion of the plight of debtors, in *Mercurius Politicus* of December 1718, as living in a "perpetual Imprisonment . . . without reprieve" and as being "lost for this World" has significance for Crusoe's condition. For if we accept Defoe's premise that "it is as reasonable to represent one kind of imprisonment by another, as it is to represent anything that really exists by that which exists not," the island may become any place where men suffer what Crusoe calls "the Silence of Life."[38] "Hence," he writes, "Man may be properly said to be *alone* in the Midst of the Crowds and Hurry of Men and Business: All the Reflections which he makes, are to himself; all that is irksome and grievous, is tasted but by his own Palat."[39]

There is something so moving about Crusoe's isolation that it inclined Tillyard to classify *Robinson Crusoe* among the few epic novels in English.[40] Some of that epic quality, I believe, arises from Defoe's tendency to identify Crusoe's experiences not only with those of all other spiritually and literally isolated individuals, but also with those of an entire nation that had been driven into the wilderness, had suffered the most brutal tortures, and had emerged with something like a victory in the end. I refer to the

"Robinson Crusoe & his boy Xury on the Coast of Guinny shooting a Lyon."
One of the six plates added to the sixth edition of ROBINSON CRUSOE *in 1722.*

Covenanters of Scotland, whose sufferings formed the basis of another epic novel, Scott's *Old Mortality*. In the January 1717 issue of *Mercurius Politicus* Defoe reported on an event that "had made some Noise" at the time, the forcing of Episcopal clergymen in Edinburgh to "bring Documents of their Ordination from such Bishops as were legally Empowered to Ordain." He then listed the names of six ministers who had been forbidden to preach. In April of that year Defoe published *Memoirs of the Church of Scotland*, a work which he may have written much earlier but which he obviously reviewed and which must still have been fresh in his mind when he was writing *Robinson Crusoe*, for here is the only other place in Defoe's writings that parallels Crusoe's spiritual experience.[41] Hunted by the Highland "Savages" after the battle of Bothwell Bridge in 1679, just as Crusoe thought he might be hunted by the savages who came to his island, the Covenanters refused to give up their faith. Houses were considered unsafe, and many took to "wandering about in Sheep-skins and Goat-skins, in Dens, and Holes, and Caves of the Earth," while the soldiers, under the command of Dalziel, set out to destroy the entire country.[42]

Defoe repeats this description of those who fled to the wilderness, clarifying his reference to Hebrews 12:37–38: "They wandered about in Sheep-skins, and Goat-skins, being destitute, afflicted, tormented; they wandered in Deserts and in Mountains, and in Dens, and Holes, and Caves of the Earth."[43] The story of the Covenanters as told by Defoe is one of mass murder and the most exquisite torture, but through it all there is something approaching joy in their willingness to lay down their lives rather than betray their beliefs:

Thus also in the Case of the Martyr'd *Maccabees*, their Persecutors pretended in Clemency to offer them their lives, if they would but take a bit of Swine's Flesh into their Mouths, tho' they did not swallow it down. But with what Abhorrence did they REFUSE! with what joy and Alacrity did they dye! I mean the primitive Christians as well as the *Maccabees*: Insomuch that the wisest of the Heathen condemn'd them as Fools; for that they cast themselves away, and lost their Lives, not for the Essential parts of Religion, but for Trifles and Circumstances of no Consequence.[44]

Defoe was plainly moved by the history of the Covenanters, and when he agrees with another writer whom he quotes on the point that persecution made them strong, it is not hard to see that he is thinking of the English Dissenters and, perhaps, of himself.

Crusoe is no Covenanter. His main interest is survival, and when that is at stake, his religious observances fall off considerably. Something of the power and force with which Defoe described the suffering Covenanters went into *Robinson Crusoe*, but so far from being a man who would go to the stake for a small point of conscience, Crusoe prides himself on ruling over the Protestant Friday, the Catholic Spaniard, and the unconverted pagan, Friday's father. The Catholic priest of the *Farther Adventures* shows an ecumenical spirit that has little in common with Hugh Mackail, the Covenanter who suffered the terrible torture of the "Boot," which crushed his leg, but who refused to violate beliefs which his conscience held sacred. Or, perhaps, the toleration permitted on Crusoe's island would allow a Hugh Mackail to hold to his beliefs.[45]

If we think in terms of Defoe's encounter with the events of his time, Crusoe appears to accept a position not far from that of the Bishop of Bangor, whose sermon teaching the English clergy that the "Kingdom of God is not of this World," brought down the wrath of the Convocation of the Anglican Church on him. At a time when John Toland's *Nazarenus*, with its suggestion that Christianity was merely a Jewish sect and Christ a mere mortal, was bringing cries of indignation from Defoe in his Tory journals, when a dispute over the Trinity involving, among others, Martin Tompkins, a dissenting minister in Defoe's own Stoke Newington and a debate in the Catholic world between the Pope and Cardinal Noailles were throwing religion into a turmoil, it is surely no accident that a lone man on an island should discover for himself an uncomplicated Christian faith based on the Bible and his need for "religious Hope" (p. 156).[46]

Defoe wrote on both sides of the Bangorian controversy. Insofar as it was a controversy in the Anglican Church, Defoe, as a Dissenter, might have felt the way he openly expressed himself about the dispute among Catholics, *"Fight Dog, Fight Bear,"* except that religious conflicts in the established church always raised political disputes. As a Tory, Defoe attacked the Bishop of Bangor; as a Whig, he defended him. As a Tory, he pointed out that in addition to being a heretic Toland was a Whig; as a Whig,

Defoe remained silent.[47] But the split in the ranks of the Dissenters must have been deeply disturbing. Defoe surely felt with the anonymous author of *An Account of the Late Proceedings of the Dissenting Ministers at Salters-Hall* that it would be best if the Dissenters did not display "Narrowness" in judging the opinions of other Christians and if they might consider that "every Man is *Orthodox* to himself."[48]

There are no disputes over the Trinity on Crusoe's island. Perhaps fiction itself forces on the writer a broadly humane position, but Crusoe's experience, even his rejection of the idea of engaging in a mass slaughter of the cannibals, leads him to a toleration of religions and nationalities. If we agree with Crusoe that "Life in general is, or ought to be, but one universal Act of Solitude," how are we to force orthodoxy on a fellow human being?[49]

VI

Crusoe commences his journal with the entry:

September 30, 1659. I poor miserable *Robinson Crusoe* being shipwreck'd, during a dreadful Storm, in the offing, came on Shore on this dismal unfortunate Island, which I call'd *the Island of Despair*, all the rest of the Ship's Company being drown'd, and my self almost dead. [P. 70]

Crusoe eventually modifies this view of his island, but there was one genuine island of despair, at least in Defoe's imagination, just about where Crusoe's island was located; it was the real island of St. Vincent, part of the Windward Islands, not far from the mouth of the Orinoco. Though the island was real, the explosion destroying the island and all its inhabitants that Defoe reported in his journals was not. Both *Mercurius Politicus* and the *Weekly Journal* contain accounts of the complete disappearance of the island and a theory of how it might have happened through the combination of an earthquake mixing nitrogen and sulphur and the force of volcanic fires meeting the sea. He compared it with an incident that occurred at Moorfields or, to make the illustration even more familiar, to throwing water on a brewer's fire and then shutting the door of the furnace on the ensuing explosion. Defoe was pleased to display his knowledge of Thomas Burnet's theories and of geology in general, but the next issue of *Mercurius*

Politicus confessed that though there was a large volcano in the middle of the island (Mount Soufrière did become violently active in 1902), the report of an explosion such as he had described had been false.[50]

But in daydreams and fantasies there can hardly be a proper island paradise without violent volcanoes and violent earthquakes. Even while he was confessing his mistake he was reporting earthquakes at the Azores and the Cape de Verde Islands. In fact, his news reports are filled with accounts of massive destruction and deaths through explosions of gunpower and lightning as well as those earthquakes and the floods described earlier. Crusoe lives in terror of being destroyed by the effect of lightning on his gunpowder, and the earthquake that strikes his island terrifies him so much that he is left "like one dead or stupify'd" (p. 80). Some earth falls into his cave and cracks appear in the beams, but he does seem to be more terrified than the occasion would warrant. Defoe's obvious preoccupation with natural disasters seems to evoke the horrors of a nightmare rather than the reality of such experiences.[51]

One example of these reports of disaster appears on 20 December 1718: "Dispatch from Corfu says lightning struck the powder in the fortress on the 21st at Night the Lightning fell upon the old Fortress of Corfu, whereby a Magazine of Powder, consisting of 400 Barrels, was blown up, and part of the Fortress with the neighbouring houses were destroyed, and amongst others the Palace of the Captain General Pesani, who was killed and buried under the Ruins, with about 14 or 1500 other Persons."[52] Again, at the seige of Melazzo in Sicily, an earthquake shakes everyone up, and thoughts of volcanoes in Sicily lead him to contemplate the final conflagration.[53] In the *Weekly Journal* of 31 January 1719 he reported a warehouse fire in London that threatened a cache of gunpowder and followed that with the discussion of a bill under consideration that would prevent storing gunpowder in the city near residences.

From accounts of mass destruction it is but a short step to reports of individual violent deaths. On 16 August 1718 he recounted the deaths of a couple struck by lightning near Oxford (an event that caused Pope to break out into three epitaphs). Similar deaths occurred in various storms at Newcastle and Lan-

cashire. But what is more impressive are the accounts of individual suicides, enough to send anyone into feelings of despair.
Hardly an issue of the *Weekly Journal* failed to contain some
strange case: a lady of wealth just about to marry a man of five
thousand pounds a year "growing Melancholy cut her Throat
from Ear to Ear;" a woman with smallpox hurls herself from the
window of a house after first picking up her two small children;[54]
and a barber who tells a customer he has just finished shaving
that, while moving the razor across his neck, he felt an irresistible
desire to cut his client's throat, rushes into a room to slash his
own belly, castrate himself, and cut his own throat. The customer, the barber's wife, and some neighbors plead with him to come
out,

but in this moment some of them perceived Blood to run out of the
Corner of the Bottom of the Door, at which, being terribly frighted, they
burst open the Door with all the speed possible, where they had the most
horrible spectacle that ever was seen, the poor wretched Creature having
mangled himself in the unaccountablist manner that ever was heard of,
Cutting several Gashes in his Belly, so that his Bowels were ready to
come out, cut a great wound in his Groyn, castrated himself entirely, and
at last cut his Throat; he was not quite Dead when they broke in, and
lived about half a quarter of an hour, but expired with the loss of Blood.[55]

Defoe's comment on one of these suicides, that of Lady Onslow,
who drowned herself, is in the form of a question: "What Discon-
tent brought this Lady to do it, who had the World as it were at
her Will, and was so effectually freed from all appearing Causes
of Dissatisfaction, it was hard to guess, and we care not to en-
quire into it."[56] If this seems a form of evasion, it shows greater
sympathy toward suicide than Defoe usually displayed.

As for Crusoe, he never falls victim to the "English Malady," as
Dr. Cheyne called melancholy—at least not for very long. But
whenever he thinks of being a "Prisoner, lock'd up with the
Eternal Bars and Bolts of the Ocean, in an uninhabited Wilderness" (p. 113), all the pleasures of his island—the "House," the
"delicious Vale" and "Bower," the feelings of certainty about his
relationship with God—disappear. He tells us how the realization
of his loneliness would "break out upon me like a Storm, and
make me wring my hands and weep like a Child" (p. 113). And
what reader can ever forget Crusoe's clenching his hands and

striking his teeth together as, wishing *"but One"* had been saved from the Spanish wreck and moved by "the Power of Imagination" (p. 188), he finds the absence of that possible companion almost too much to bear.

Some of the problems with recent interpretations of *Robinson Crusoe* along strictly religious lines may be found in their incompatibility with the experience of the book itself.[57] Religion is part of Crusoe's life. It gives him a rationale for what he is already doing in striving to survive. It gives him hope, and before the arrival of Friday, it gives him a being with whom he can hold an imaginary dialogue. But when his religious duties slacken, Crusoe is Crusoe still. He is a man imprisoned on a real and symbolic island. And when we speak of Defoe in terms of prisons, we are dealing with an experience he knew well. Like Dickens's Old Dorrit, he must have known that "jail rot" which leaves its permanent psychological scars.[58]

For these reasons, books about isolation and imprisonment may tell us more about *Robinson Crusoe* than tomes of casuistry. Studies of such an experience describe the typical pattern of the isolate—the change from fear to frequent hallucinations, and eventually, if the individual is to survive, to an "introspective or internal resilience" which enables the victim, as one writer put it, to "acquire a deep-set conviction that [he] will master the experience; [he] become[s] highly motivated and devote[s] most of [his] waking hours to acquiring some new scientific or technical skill."[59] One of the most intriguing of these accounts of isolation comes from Christopher Burney, who was put in solitary confinement by the Germans during World War II. Burney describes how he gradually came to half enjoy his experience and how he succeeded in creating an infinite variety in the confines of his cell. "We are narrow men," he writes, "twisted men, smooth and nicely rounded men, and poets; but whatever we are, we have our shape, and we preserve best in the experience of many things. If the reach of experience is suddenly confined, and we are left with only a little food for thought and feeling, we are apt to take the few objects that offer themselves and ask a whole catalogue of questions about them."[60]

Now Crusoe, unlike some of the subjects in experiments on isolation, does not suffer sensory deprivation. His island provides him abundant variety, but he is confined in both a real and psychological sense. When he explores his island, he feels a real happiness in returning to his "Home," even though it is on the least attractive part of the island. "Imagination," writes Burney, "is an optimist."[61] Whatever else Defoe gives us in *Robinson Crusoe*, he certainly provides us with a picture of imagination at work, creating, ordering, and absorbing the world around him. If his triumph over the island is mostly an economic conquest, it is an imaginative conquest as well.

Although I have devoted this chapter to showing the ways in which Defoe transmuted the materials of life into fiction, I cannot end it without addressing the overall pattern of myth that provides the envelope for Defoe's realistic fantasies. Obviously Crusoe does not entirely fit the pattern of the ideal hero of myth.[62] But if Defoe created his work in such a manner as to resist the easy identification between reader and hero to be found in romances, he provided enough of a pattern to allow the reader to force him into that role. Crusoe comes along at a moment of historical transition when the values of the past are open to question. Young men like him and his brothers run off to the army or go to sea and abandon the safe ways of living in their world. Crusoe's adventures and his stay on the island may be seen as a punishment, yet it is also a quest after meaning. With the guidance of Providence, Crusoe rejects his past in order to discover something about himself and the world that he had forgotten or never knew clearly. As Mircea Eliade suggests in discussing the reasons for the presence of initiatory themes in Western literature, "Even if the initiatory character of these ordeals is not apprehended as such, it remains true nonetheless that man becomes *himself* only after having solved a series of desperately difficult and even dangerous situations; that is, after having undergone "tortures" and "death," followed by an awakening to another life, qualitatively different because regenerated."[63] Crusoe's triumph over the island is always endangered by the threat of the wilderness, but he creates his own empire by making a conquest of the island's economic resources and makes himself worthy of success by his spiritual growth. His wealth would have given him the position in England that would have been equivalent to the satisfactions of his island life, but he is unable to endure the translation of his success into such a worldly reality. Like Tennyson's Ulysses, who has more than a share of Crusoe in him, he embarks on his travels once more, not to seek the transcendence of his island life but to escape its banal, civilized equivalent.

Crusoe's afterlife as a mythic figure is the subject of a book rather than a paragraph, but we should be aware of the many texts through which we read *Robinson Crusoe* now.[64] And we should also realize that as a social artifact, Defoe's book has shaped our perception of the world. At Genoa, in the *lazaretto* where he must live in isolation and provide for his comforts as well as on the island of Saint-Pierre in the middle of the Lake of Bienne, Switzerland, Rousseau's imagination seizes on his role as a new Robinson shaping a new world and discovering his true self.[65] And if the novel was never the same after Crusoe's account, could genuine relations of shipwrecks ever be without its echo of Crusoe's experiences? For example, in *A Voyage to the South Seas in His Majesty's Ship the Wager in the Years 1740–1741* by John Bulkeley and John Cummins, the terrifying accounts of starvation and danger are often so close to sections of the two parts of *Robinson Crusoe* that one would have to conclude that these sailors tended to view their experiences through a fairly vivid recollection of Defoe's novel.[66]

Bachelard, whose work I have found useful for this study, quotes one of Van Gogh's letters to his brother in which he writes that we should "retain something of the original character of a Robinson Crusoe. Make and remake everything oneself, make a 'supplementary gesture' toward each object, give another facet to the polished reflections, all of which are so many boons the imagination confers upon us by making us aware of the House's inner growth. To have an active day I keep saying to myself, 'Every morning I must give a thought to Saint Robinson.'"[67] For all the time spent discussing the realism of *Robinson Crusoe*, we would miss everything if we did not feel the force behind his hero's daydreams. I am not suggesting that Crusoe's world was like Kafka's version of *Don Quixote*, an hallucination concocted by a new Sancho Panza. But the way Defoe turned the materials of his journalism and his own experience into fiction reveals a great visionary realist at work.[68]

3

History, Ideology, and the Method
of Defoe's Historical Fiction

If within seven or ten Years People can scarce prevail upon themselves to think regularly of Things past, or to entertain just Notions of Actions, or of the Persons that perform'd them; what must be the Case forty or fifty Years afterwards, when the Men whose Memories could correct the Injustice of Historians, shall be gone off the Stage, and Men are at liberty to add or diminish, as they please, in the Story of Times past?

Actions of great Men, not unalterably recorded at the time on which they were perform'd, and recorded by an Authority unquestion'd; are expos'd to the Mercy of Posterity, in a most scandalous and unhappy Manner. This is evident from the Histories of the few Ages since Queen Elizabeth's Reign, of which it may indeed be said, with some affliction, that we have not one faithful impartial History left; nor anything extant, . . . with sufficient Authority, and from which another Writer may justify his Ideas of Things then in Agitation. DEFOE, *Applebee's Original Weekly Journal, 18 August 1722*

SIR WALTER SCOTT, with whose fiction almost all studies of the historical novel commence, classified Defoe's two great historical novels, *Memoirs of a Cavalier* and *A Journal of the Plague Year*, together under the category of works concerned with "great national convulsions, . . . tales which are sure, when even moderately well told, to arrest the attention"; and his description of the latter work as "that particular class of composition which hovers between romance and history," was a classification intended to cover the Cavalier's account of the wars of the seventeenth century as well.[1] Scott rightly remarked that both works had been mistaken for "a real production of a real personage," but in this they share the fate of much fictional narrative written in the first person. If Defoe's use of that ancient device of pretending to take his story from an old manuscript is given additional force by his astonishing stylistic powers, we should not be prevented from seeing the convention for what it is. Neither work contains the traditional nineteenth-century convention of the love story; nevertheless both are historical novels. I am not the first person to make this claim,[2] but I may be the first to suggest how the historical visions of the Cavalier and the Saddler are shaped by Defoe's peculiar vision and intention.

I am not going to pretend that the problem of separating history from fiction is simple. Recent studies of historical method have thrown doubt on either the possibility or even the desirability of achieving a genuinely objective history. Writers like J. H. Hexter and W. B. Gallie have approached historical narrative in a manner not very different from that of a literary critic, while Hayden White has argued that historians are almost always treating texts of one kind or another rather than events.[3] Even the distinction between the kind of "truth" in history and that insisted on by novelists like Joseph Conrad tends to blur in dealing with historical fiction.[4] In his book on the historical novel, Herbert Butterfield argued many years ago that "statesmen and kings and scientists . . . are not shut out of the novel, but the novelist's interest in them is not an interest in the statesmanship, or in the rule, or in the science but in the whole personality of the man behind these, and his theme is still a human heart caught into the world and entangled in time and circumstance."[5] But in this he falls into the trap of conceiving novels as necessarily involved in character portrayals and romantic intrigues. He is on much better grounds when he distinguishes between the ways in which the historian and the novelist use their materials when he concludes: "With a set of facts about the social conditions of England in the Middle Ages the historian will seek to make a generalisation, to find a formula; the novelist will seek a different sort of synthesis and will try to reconstruct a world, to particularise, to catch a glimpse of human nature."[6] Yet even this statement fails to take into account the genuine interest in history for history's sake to be found in writers like Defoe, Scott, and Tolstoy. In order to understand *Memoirs of a Cavalier* and *A Journal of the Plague Year* as fiction, it will help to understand Defoe's approach to the use of history in his fiction, to the meaning of a given historical event for his own time, and to history as a discipline.

I

For the purpose of this discussion, I will begin with a scene in *Memoirs of a Cavalier*. The narrator is in Lyons on a Sunday evening in late May or early April of 1630, when he witnesses a riot over bread and taxes. The magistrates choose to ignore the crowds at first.

> But on *Sunday* Night, about Midnight, we was waked by a prodigious Noise in the Street; I jumpt out of Bed, and running to the Window, I saw the Street as full of Mob as it could hold, some armed with Musquets and Halbards, marched in very good Order; others in disorderly Crouds, all shouting and crying out *du Paix le Roy*, and the like; One that led a great Party of this Rabble carried a Load of Bread upon the Top of a Pike, and other Lesser Loaves, signifying the Smallness of their Bread, occasioned by Dearness.
>
> By Morning this Croud was gathered to a great Heighth, they run roving over the whole City, shut up all the Shops, and forced all the People to join with them from thence; they went up to the Castle, and renewing the Clamour, a strange Consternation seized all the Princes.
>
> They broke open the Doors of the Officers, Collectors of the new Taxes, and plundered their Houses, and had not the Persons themselves fled in time they had been very ill treated.7

The riot is finally quelled by the Queen Mother, who promises the mob redress, but not until the Cavalier is stopped by a "Party of Mutineers" and dragged back before the Queen Mother as a spy (pp. 16–17). From this adventure, the Cavalier says he developed "an Aversion to popular Tumults all my Life after," and that it partly explains why he eventually was to fight for King Charles I (p. 17). At the same time, he remarks that the Queen Mother handled the crowd brilliantly and that she "understood much better than King *Charles*, the Management of Politics, and the Clamours of the People." Thus the experience of the riot is used to explain the character of Defoe's fictional narrator and to make one of the apparently reluctant criticisms of Charles I that are to be found throughout the work by the king's purported admirer. The riot forms part of the pattern of disorder that underlies every historical event, but at this point in Defoe's novel the Cavalier reveals a response to the inconveniences he has suffered rather than any reaction to the sufferings of the people that caused the riot. He will become more sympathetic to human suffering by the end of his narrative.

Defoe's main source for the experiences of the Cavalier in France and Italy was Jean Le Clerc's *Life of the Famous Cardinal-Duke de Richelieu*, a work that he was reading during the period of his life when he was a spy for Robert Harley in Scotland and deeply involved in the political events that led to the Union of England and Scotland. But all Le Clerc states is that the taxes had made the people "discontented" and that "there had been some Seditions in Burgundy, and also a Commotion at Lyons, although the Queens were present, the People refusing to pay the new Taxes."[8]

Although some other source may be possible,[9] Defoe actually drew his feeling for the riot in Lyons from rioting in Edinburgh, which he recounted to Harley in a letter on 24 October 1706. He described how the first actions of the mob had been suppressed and how, thinking the streets safe enough around nine o'clock at night to get to his lodgings, he barely avoided the violence that followed:

I had not been Long There but I heard a Great Noise and looking Out Saw a Terrible Multitude Come up the High street with A Drum at the head of Them shouting and swearing and Cryeing Out all scotland would stand together, No Union, No Union, English Dogs, and the like.

I Can Not Say to you I had No Apprehensions, Nor was Monsr *De Witt* quite Out of my Thoughts, and perticularly when a part of This Mob fell upon a Gentleman who had Discretion little Enough to say something that Displeased them just Undr my Window.

He Defended himself bravely and Call'd Out lustily also for help to the Guard, who being within Hearing and Ready Drawn up in Close Ordr in the street, advanc't, Rescued the Gentleman, and took the person he was Grappld with prisoner.

The City was by this time in a Terrible fright. The Guards were Insulted and stoned as they stood, the Mob put out all the lights, no body could stir in the streets, and not a light be seen in a windo' for fear of stones.[10]

The intent of this passage is vividness and immediacy. As in *Memoirs of a Cavalier*, the cries of the mob give the reader the sense of hearing the event just as the beating of the Gentleman and the stoning of the Guard force us to feel the experience. A special mood is conveyed through the sudden appearance of the mob in the street at night, through verbs of action, and through comments on the writer's feeling of anxiety, which, he suggests, is the collective emotion of the entire city.

When he transferred this scene to his lengthy, formal *History of the Union* (1709), it appeared in a context involving an analysis of the composition of the mob. Many who should have supported the Union were, for various reasons, against it. Except for stating that he was an eyewitness of the events, Defoe eliminated himself from the action. He lengthened the paragraphs, but for the most part he retained his account to Harley as a bit of vivid narrative in a general analysis of causes and a chronicle of daily events. The sense of anxiety apparent in the letter is made more explicit: "People went up and down wandering and amazed, expecting every day strange Events . . . They could not be clear for the Union; yet they saw Death at the Door, in its breaking off; Death to their Liberty, to their Religion, and to their Country."[11]

In preparing his account of the yet more violent Glasgow riots for *The History of the Union*, Defoe presented the reader with a sympathetic picture of the confusion of the common people. They were worked up to "Excesses, Madness, and Distraction." Many of the leaders of the Presbyterians were opposed to the Union. "Who then," he asks, "can censure the poor depending, uninformed and abused People?" He then proceeded to an account of the Glasgow mob, their breaking into the house of the Provost, and his escape by hiding in a bed folded into the wall:

The Rabble was now fully Master of the Town, they ranged the Streets, and did what they pleased; No Magistrate durst show his Face to them, they challenged People as they walk'd the Streets with this Question, *Are you for the Union?* And no Man durst own it, but at their extremest Hazard.

The next thing they did, was to search for Arms in all the Houses of those, that had appeared for the Union; And first they went to the Dean of the Guild, and, upon his refusing to give them his Arms, they took them away by Force; They stopt here a little, but having given out, that they would search the Houses of all that were for the Union, the Magistrates Assembled, and Considering, that, if the Citizens were Disarmed, and the Rabble possest of their Weapons, they might, in the next place, possess their Houses, Wives and Wealth, at their Command; and that it was better to Defend themselves now, then be Murdered and Plundered in cold Blood; They resolved therefore to raise some Strength, to oppose this Violence.[12]

This passage has many of the qualities of the scene that Defoe witnessed in Edinburgh. The reader is directed forward in time by adverbs like "now . . . next . . . first . . . upon . . . in the next place," and moved about in space by verbs of movement, "ranged . . . walk'd . . . went . . . took." But here Defoe was not an eyewitness; he was not in Glasgow at the time of the riots, and the scene, like that in *Memoirs of a Cavalier,* is recreated to give the same vividness he achieved for the Edinburgh riots. Since in both places he was obviously generalizing from his experience of the psychology of riots, in what sense is his account of the Glasgow riots different from fiction?

An answer to such a question would have been almost as difficult to come by in Defoe's time as it would be today. La Mothe le Vayer gave full expression to historical Pyrrhonism as early as 1668,[13] and a strain of doubt about history may be found throughout the eighteenth century. Dr. Johnson, for example, remarked that "all the colouring, all the philosophy of history is conjecture," and complained of the "shallow stream of thought in history."[14] He objected particularly to passages such as the following from Sir John Dalrymple's *Memoirs of Great Britain and Ireland* depicting the feelings of James II on learning of the invasion of William III: "He turned pale and stood motionless: the letter dropped from his hand: His past errors, his future dangers, rush at once upon his thoughts; he strove to conceal his perturbation, but, in doing so, betrayed it."[15] Such readings of inner thoughts were indeed conjecture. Everyone agreed that firsthand accounts were always preferable, but they too often took on the character of the writer, his egotism, his point of view. That the writer of a memoir was the hero of his own romance was a commonplace of the times. And what Hume remarked about the accuracy of reports on miracles might easily be applied to almost any historical event.[16]

Defoe claimed (surely with some exaggeration) to have read every historical account available, and his history-reading Cavalier resembles his ideal gentleman in this respect. In his early work, *The Storm* (1704), which, as Scott remarked, has affinities with both *Memoirs of a Cavalier* and *A Journal of the Plague Year* in that it treated a national disaster,[17] Defoe stated what he considered to be the job of the impartial historian:

> *If I judge right, Tis the Duty of an Historian to set every thing in its own Light, and to convey matter of fact upon its legitimate Authority, and no other: I mean thus, (for I wou'd be as explicit as I can) That where a Story is vouch'd to him with sufficient Authority, he ought to give the World the special Testimonial of its proper Voucher, or else he is not just to the Story: and where it comes without such sufficient Authority, he ought to say so; otherwise he is not just to himself. In the first Case he injures the History, by leaving it doubtful where it might be confirm'd past all manner of question; in the last he injures his own Reputation, by taking upon himself the Risque, in case it proves a Mistake, of having the World charge him with a Forgery.[18]*

Scott considered *The Storm* a dull rendering of an exciting event, lacking Defoe's usual imagination.[19] And so it was, but it was also typical of the scrupulousness about evidence that was common to historians and antiquarians at that time. As Arnaldo Momigliano states, "What characterizes the writing of history in the late seventeenth and early eighteenth centuries is the large number of historians whose main concern was to ascertain the truth of each event by the best methods of research."[20]

But Defoe was a propagandist and a journalist more than he was a historian. For all his effort at collecting accounts about the tempest that struck England on 24 November 1703, for all his attack on works that change history into "meer Romance," and for all his signing himself "The Ages Humble Servant," Defoe was not one to omit his own views from his accounts. He tended to approach history as a "Whig historian," reading the present into the past in terms of the progress of liberty as evidence of the workings of Providence in the world. As an economic historian, he could strike the gloomy posture of what Kant called historical "terrorism."[21] Yet he was at his best describing the growth and progress of English industry. He was certainly not above distorting history to suit his own purposes. His *Memoirs of the Church of*

Scotland (1717) blatantly favors the cause of the Covenanters and shows the Anglicans in the darkest colors. Scott politely calls it "incorrect";[22] a more modern critic compares it to the type of propaganda that was produced under Adolf Hitler.[23]

Yet Defoe's *History of the Union,* from which I have quoted, is a fairly scrupulous narrative of the events leading to the joining of the two nations. Defoe expresses his opinions about various events in sections labelled "Observations," which are marked off from the factual minutes of the debates. He is hardly impartial, favoring the Union and disparaging the forces working against it. But he does strike the historian's pose of general sympathy for well-meaning people of all sides. And so far from being outraged by the mob, as was his Cavalier, Defoe is sympathetic:

> It was not for the poor People, to distinguish the Original of Causes and Things, nor who was at the Bottom of these Rumours [that the Union would have terrible consequences]; it was not for them to distinguish the Hand of *Joab* in all this; whether *Jacobite* or Papist was the Original of this Matter, was not for them to examine; They saw their Superiors joyning in the same Complaint, and every Party saw some of their respective Chiefs embark'd.
>
> The common People could look no further; the Episcopal Poor saw their Curates Tooth and Nail against it; The Ignorant and Indifferent Poor, saw their *Jacobite* Land-Lords and Masters Railing at it; and which was worse still, the Honest Presbyterian poor People saw some of their Gentlemen, and such as they had remarked and noticed *to be Hearty Presbyterians,* yet appearing against it;—Who then can censure the poor depending, uninformed and abused People.?[24]

The Cavalier's lack of compassion at the beginning of *Memoirs of a Cavalier* is part of the novel's exploitation of character. The compassion for the confused people of Scotland is part of the pattern of history that Defoe imposes on his work.

Of course that pattern is itself a kind of fiction. Defoe even gives *The History of the Union* a plot roughly similar to that of *A Journal of the Plague Year.* He remarks that "the whole Nation seemed as in an Agony, the Enemies of the Union went about Bemoaning *Scotland,* and Sighing as they called it, for the Dying Constitution, and . . . 'for their Dying Country'."[25] The spectacle of a city or a country in crisis and triumphing over its difficulties is obviously a plot that fiction may share with history, and as one contributor to *History and Theory* has suggested, such parallels are not uncommon.[26] But surrounded as this section is with documentation, no one would ever mistake *The History of the Union* for a work of fiction. The thrust of Defoe's vision, even in narrative passages, moves the reader toward the event rather than toward the individual participants or to an excessive awareness of the historical narrator.

I want to end this part of my discussion of history and fiction with a brief summary of Defoe's attitudes toward history and then move on to a discussion of the novels themselves. As we have seen, he had a tendency toward collecting raw data and documents; and like Samuel Pufendorf, he preferred to treat relatively current events and to stress socioeconomic analysis. He was mainly interested in causes, or what he called "the strange Circulation of Causes," and he liked to show his skill at narratives of battles or disasters, a skill that Steele had found wanting in most historians.[27] He tended toward what Nietzsche called "Monumental History," history that turned on the brilliance of one hero[28]—a Gustavus Adolphus, a William III, a Marlborough. But he also believed that heroic figures were at the service of Providence and would emerge when needed.

In many ways, he shared historical attitudes with his Italian contemporary, Giambattista Vico. Like Vico, he believed that the workings of second causes in history along with human free will would validate the providential course of history. What one writer has called Vico's "acquiescence in actuality"[29] has its counterpart in the ideology underlying Defoe's realism; both worked from the real event to Providence. And most important, like Vico, he had faith in fiction as exemplifying history. To introduce fictional events into his *History of the Pirates* in the form of a contrast between the Communist, Captain Misson, and the practical colonialist, Captain Tew, was to force history to do its job by way of providing examples.[30] Not that Defoe possessed Vico's profound insight into language and myth, but no one can write a great historical novel without having thought long and hard about the meaning of history itself. As a historical novelist, Defoe was far from the naive artist that some critics have made him out to be.

II

Defoe would never have mistaken *Memoirs of a Cavalier* for genuine history, and the preface suggests as much. While claiming that the manuscript was authentic, the emphasis of the preface by the manuscript's fictitious editor is on the brilliant writing and the general accuracy of the materials when compared with known historical accounts:

> As it is not proper to trace them any farther, so neither is there any need to trace them at all, to give Reputation to the Story related, seeing the Actions here mentioned have a sufficient Sanction from all the Histories of the Times to which they relate, with this Addition, that the admirable Manner of relating them, and the wonderful Variety of Incidents, with which they are beautified in the Course of a private Gentleman's Story, add such Delight in the reading, and give such a Lustre, as well to the Accounts themselves, as to the Person who was the Actor; and no Story, we believe, extant in the World, ever came abroad with such Advantages. [P. vii]

The author of the preface proceeds to praise the battle accounts and to assure the reader that *"the Story is inimitably told"* (p. viii). The suggestion that there may be a sequel is hardly intended to give the reader the feeling that he is reading a genuine account, and the note struck at the end is the kind of advertisement that might be expected for a work of fiction. *"Nothing more can invite than the Story it self,"* he writes, *"which when the Reader enters into, he will find it very hard to get out of, 'till he has gone thro' it"* (p. xi).

The shape of *Memoirs of a Cavalier* is essentially novelistic. The Cavalier does not tell a series of continual adventures but sets up two experiences by way of contrast and interplay: his participation in the events of the Thirty Years War that saw Gustavus Adolphus triumph over the enemies of the Protestant princes of Germany until his death at the battle of Lutzen in 1632, and his involvement in the actions leading up to the English Civil War until his surrender with the king's forces in 1645. Although there are introductory passages involving the wars in Italy and connecting passages between these two blocks of time, the Cavalier's adventures in fighting the enemies of Gustavus Adolphus and Charles I stand as separate experiences, each commenting on the other.

The reason for this artistic decision has something to do with

the political impulse behind the work. The common interpretation of Defoe's reasons for writing *Memoirs of a Cavalier* is that he
was taking advantage of contemporary interest in Charles XII, the
apparent successor to Gustavus Adolphus as Sweden's military
genius, but the most immediate cause may be discovered in Defoe's championing the Protestant cause in Europe and the Dissenting cause in England.[31] Both were under attack at the time
Defoe was writing.

In its issue of January 1720, the *Present State of Europe* reported
that the Elector of the Palatine had begun to persecute his Protestant subjects in direct violation of the Treaty of Westphalia, the
treaty guaranteeing Protestant liberties that Gustavus Adolphus
had given his life to defend:

This was too flagrant to be indur'd, and therefore the Kings of Great-
Britain and Prussia, the States-General, and the Landgrave of Hesse-
Cassel, sent their Ministers to signifie to the Elector Palatine, That unless
he redress'd the Grievances of his Protestant Subjects, they would use
Reprisals upon the Roman Catholicks in their Dominions. They have
begun the same in some Places, but this has not yet been able to induce
the Palatine Court to do the Justice desir'd of them, and the Empire
seems to be threaten'd with Intestine Troubles upon that Account, if the
Emperor, who lyes under so many Obligations to the Protestants does
not effectually interpose his Authority, to compel these bold Infringers of
Solemn Treaties, to give Satisfaction to the Injur'd, and restore all Things
on the Foot of these Treaties.[32]

The same issue reported the resolutions passed by the represen-
tatives of the Protestant states at Ratisbon insisting on restoration
of the provisions of the Treaty of Westphalia and quoted the
comment of the Elector on possible reprisals against Catholics to
the effect that "he could not but pity the Innocent who would
suffer thereby."[33]

The suggestion of another Thirty Years War on the horizon
could not help reminding those who knew their history of the
horrors of that conflict, which had turned large parts of Germany
into a desert. News reports over the following months, however,
showed continuing attacks on the liberties of Protestants. *Memoirs
of a Cavalier* was announced for publication on 24 May 1720, by
which time matters had calmed down considerably. In April the
emperor agreed to follow the Treaty of Westphalia, although not

without telling the Diet of the Deputies of the Confession of Augsburg that he did not like their tone in threatening reprisals against Catholics.[34] Great Britain and her allies had applied pressure on the Elector Palatine, and he had yielded. A new religious war in Europe had been avoided, but not before Defoe had composed his account of the Cavalier's experience under the hero of the Protestant cause.

The idea of contrasting the two wars may have been the product of a debate between Thomas Sherlock, Dean of Chichester, and Benjamin Hoadly, Bishop of Bangor, over the Test and Corporation Acts—the laws that prevented Dissenters from serving in local or national employments. With seeming reluctance but obvious relish, Sherlock reminded his readers in 1718 of the horrors perpetrated by the ancestors of the Dissenters during the Civil War and Interregnum:

'Tis with reluctance that I enter into this part of the argument; and I wish I cou'd draw a curtain before the oppressions and calamities which the Nation suffered under, in that long hour of darkness. But shou'd I be silent, yet almost every Gentleman's family wears still the scars of the frenzy; and can name the *Ancestor*, who *lost* his *life*, the *Estate* that was *sequestred*, the *House* that was *pillaged* or *pulled down*: And this too was acted under the pretence of making way for the *free profession* of the *Gospel*; of which however there was hardly any visible sign in the Kingdom, except only this; *That our Kings were bound in chains, and our Nobles with links of iron.*[35]

Although Sherlock admitted "that *Religion* was not the *whole* of that unhappy rupture between the King and his People," he suggested that matters like *"Civil Rights"* might have been exaggerated by Clarendon as a cause of the conflict, for such rights would have been secured without a struggle "had not the pretences of Religion and Enthusiasm mix'd themselves in the quarrel, and put the Nation into such a *Fever*, that nothing but the loss of Blood cou'd recover them again to their cool senses."[36]

In his reply, Hoadly accused Sherlock of giving a false picture of the Civil War and a *"Utopian Account"* of the Restoration. Identifying Sherlock with the entire breed of bad historians, Hoadly remarked that "They will rather unnecessarily *Coin* a piece of *History*, and Embellish it with all the *Flowres* They can strew upon

it, than avoid any fair Opportunity of *Self-Contradiction.*"[37] Sherlock retorted that the Bishop of Bangor's version of history was no
more than his "peculiar Dream."[38] But Sherlock also had to defend himself against other antagonists. James Peirce reminded
him that if he wanted examples of a religious body attempting to
destroy the state, he would be better off looking at the behavior of
some Anglicans in 1688 and 1715 than at the Civil War,[39] and
Moses Lowman cited chapter and verse in Clarendon against his
version of events.[40]

Peirce's easy move to present events from what he regarded as
distant history suggests how much contemporaries might have
agreed, in an odd way, with the varied arguments of Croce,
Heidegger, and others that all history is necessarily present history. As José Ortega y Gasset wrote, "That Past is not because it
happened to others but because it forms part of our present, of
what we are in the form of having been, because, in short, it is *our
past.*"[41] The *Memoirs of a Cavalier* is very much about the religious
wars of the seventeenth century, but it is also about the threat to
religious freedom in Defoe's own England and Europe. If Defoe
seems to be overreacting, it is because he seemed at this time to
fear an impending catastrophe. The Dissenters had fallen into
warring factions after the Salters Hall meetings in 1719, just a
short time after the Anglicans had done the same following Benjamin Hoadly's sermon on the relation of the church to the state.
Weavers had been rioting in the streets, and Defoe had under-
taken to defend their cause as a clear case of the rich oppressing
the poor.[42] A new Jacobite revolt had just fizzled, but not without
the threat of strong support from Spain and Sweden. The stock
market was moving rapidly toward the disaster of the South Sea
Bubble, and Defoe could see ahead to a real plague coming as
punishment for the plague of avarice. In *The Anatomy of Exchange
Alley* (1719) he resorted to prophecy: "The Truth is, it has been
foretold by cunning Men, who often see what can't be hid, that
these Men by a Mass of Money which they command of other
Peoples, as well as their own, will, in Time, ruin the Jobbing-
Trade. But 'twill be only like a general Visitation, where all Dis-
tempers are swallow'd up in the Plague, like a common Calamity,
that makes Enemies turn Friends, and drowns less Grievances in
the general Deluge" (pp. 40–41). And in a pamphlet that ap-

peared just before the publication of *Memoirs of a Cavalier*, Defoe, identifying himself as "one who has no Dependance on Church, State, or Exchange-Alley,"[43] attacked Archbishop Laud and the Church as the true cause of England's ills during the reign of Charles I. As if in direct answer to Sherlock's charge, he remarked: "This makes some people wonder with what Confidence our High Clergy can bellow out *Forty One*, and not put their Followers in mind, that their Fathers, the Clergy, . . . were the principal Cause of the Miseries of those Days."[44] Defoe's solution to the problems posed by what he calls an "Army of at least fifty Thousand black Coats in constant and full Pay"[45] is simple: eliminate their jobs.

Now the tone of *Memoirs of a Cavalier* is a different matter entirely. Defoe's hero is not one of Defoe's rogues or an *alter ego*, as has sometimes been suggested, but a gentleman searching for a proper calling and a just cause to espouse. He does not like to speak about his private life, criticizing the Parliament's publication of the king's private correspondence after the letters fell into their hands at the Battle of Naseby, but he is willing to speak of his feelings and attitudes. Like Colonel Jack, he undergoes an extensive change throughout his narrative. He starts his adventures on the continent by killing a man in a duel, and he registers as little emotion over this as over the wars in Italy. His description of the conflict in Germany contains accounts of death and butchery, but he seems to regard the excitement of war as more important than the suffering he perceives. Only the taking of Magdenburgh by Tilly's forces moves him: "the Slaughter was very dreadful, we could see the poor People in Crowds driven down the Streets, flying from the Fury of the Soldiers who followed butchering them as fast as they could, . . . the desparate Wretches would throw themselves into the River, where Thousands of them perished, especially Women and Children; several Men that could swim got over to our Side, where the Soldiers not heated with Fight gave them Quarter, and took them up" (p. 46). This is a moment not uncommon in Defoe's fiction when the failure of language makes a description more intense. Although his account is vivid enough, the Cavalier states, "I cannot pretend to describe the Cruelty of this Day" (p. 47).

But while this battle gives him an aversion to the emperor's soldiers and his cause, it does not turn him from his idea of becoming a soldier. In fighting with his hero, Gustavus Adolphus, he discovers what his father doubted he would find—a *"War . . . worth while for a Man to appear in"* (p. 5). But if he worships Gustavus as his hero—a man of generosity, who rewards talent wherever he finds it, promoting brave, common soldiers on the battlefield—he still describes with relatively little emotion battles in which entire garrisons are put to the sword. He admires prudence and caution, praising the magistrates of Leipzig for their wisdom in storing supplies for a siege, arguing that the Swedes neglected these ideals of Gustavus and thereby lost the Battle of Nordlingen. But he is not cautious in his own actions, and he finds the patient wars of Prince Maurice unbearably dull.

When the Cavalier has returned to his own country and is ready to engage in the wars with Scotland that preceded the English Civil War, he has learned a little about the suffering that wars may cause, but he is restless enough to fight in any war that may come along. Much of criticism of his own attitude is the result of hindsight:

The Cloud that seemed to threaten most was from *Scotland.* My Father, who had made himself Master of the Arguments on both Sides, used to be often saying, he feared there was some about the King who exasperated him too much against the *Scots,* and drove things too high. For my part, I confess I did not much trouble my Head with the Cause; but all my Fear was, they would not fall out, and we should have no Fighting. I have often reflected since, that I ought to have known better, that had seen how the most flourishing Provinces of *Germany* were reduced to the most miserable Condition that ever any Country in the World was, by the Ravagings of Soldiers, and the Calamities of War. [P. 135]

Unlike most of Defoe's heroes, the Cavalier learns his lessons slowly.

In all of this, Defoe's propaganda was well served. The Cavalier reports that the war with the Scots was really "a Church War" and that the king was "besieged with clergymen" (p. 137). A courageous gentleman, whose opinion is validated by our being informed that he died for the king, is given the answer to Sherlock in a conversation with the Cavalier: "A Pox on these Priests, says he, 'tis for them the King has raised this Army, and put his Friends to a vast Charge" (p. 139). Although the Cavalier later realizes that the churchmen were wise in advising the King not to fight, he never comes to a high opinion of the clergy's role in the war: "My old Comerades and Fellow-soldiers in *Germany* were some *with us*, some *against us*, as their Opinions happened to differ in Religion. For my part, I confess I had not much Religion in me, at that time; but I thought Religion rightly practiced on both Sides would have made us all better Friends; and therefore sometimes I begin to think, that both the Bishops of our Side, and the Preachers on theirs, made Religion rather *the Pretence* than *the Cause* of the War" (p. 185). But despite Defoe's anticlericism at this time, and his interest in throwing the causes of the war more particularly on the Anglican clergy, the dominant force of the book is in the direction of reconciliation.

The burden of this spirit is carried by the Cavalier himself who looks back on his behavior at the beginning of the war as thoughtless:

I confess, when I went into Arms at the Beginning of this War, I never troubled my self to examine Sides: I was glad to hear the Drums beat for Soldiers; as if I had been a meer *Swiss*, that had not car'd which Side went up or down, so I had my Pay. I went as eagerly and blindly about my Business, as the meanest Wretch that listed in the Army; nor had I the least compassionate Thought for the Miseries of my native Country, 'till after the Fight at *Edgehill*. I had known as much, and perhaps more than most in the Army, what it was to have an Enemy ranging in the Bowels of a Kingdom; I had seen the most flourishing Provinces of *Germany* reduced to perfect Desarts, and the voracious *Crabats*, with inhuman Barbarity, quenching the Fires of the plundered Villages with the Blood of the Inhabitants. [P. 138]

His speculation on whether his experiences in Germany had hardened him to all feeling about death and misery prepares the reader for his awakening to the misery of a civil war.

The conversion does indeed come after Edgehill. He tells of his "unaccountable Sadness" at learning what war is like when Englishmen are involved:

It grieved me to the Heart, even in the Rout of our Enemies, to see the Slaughter of them; and even in the Fight, to hear a Man cry for Quarter in

English, moved me to a Compassion which I had never been used to; nay, sometimes it looked to me as if some of my own Men had been beaten; and when I heard a Soldier cry, *O God, I am shot,* I looked behind me to see which of my own Troop was fallen. Here I saw my self at the cutting of the Throats of my Friends; and indeed some of my near Relations. [Pp. 184–85]

The Cavalier proceeds to excuse some of his actions as justified by the laws of war, but the reader knows better. He remarks that the English "Common People" might not have minded the raids of Prince Rupert, if they could have seen the "Ruin and Depopulation, Murthers, Ravishments, and Barbarities, which I have seen even among Protestant Armies abroad in Germany" (p. 188). That he immediately apologizes for seeming to suggest that he is offering "these greater Barbarities to justify lesser Actions" (p. 189) reveals that he too knows better. His point is a halfhearted one—that "this War was managed with as much Humanity on both Sides as could be expected, . . . considering the Animosity of the Parties" (p. 189).

The fact is that Defoe's sources told of bitter resistance by the German Boors to the armies raiding their farms,[46] and the Cavalier tells of one occasion when a woman successfully resisted a raiding party and drove off the troops. But this action has certain comic overtones compared to the Cavalier's murder of everyone—men, women, and children—in a private house. He states evasively, "I cannot say no Blood was shed in a Manner too rash . . . but our Case was desperate" (p. 234). At Leicester, he and his troops give quarter to no one, and while justifying his actions as acceptable according to the laws of warfare, he is obviously uncomfortable with his part in the war (p. 274).

His discomfort is revealed mainly in a tendency to blame others—the king for failing to be resolute and for listening to priests, Prince Rupert for charging through the lines of the enemy in a manner that wins one part of the field but loses the battle, the city of London for providing an inexhaustible supply of money and men for the Parliament's armies. He is particularly hard on Prince Rupert, though it would appear from his own confession that he engaged in some of Rupert's wild charges and that he was as eager to engage the enemy in a foolhardy manner as anyone else. This tendency to rid himself of any guilt he might feel prepares the reader for what almost amounts to a shift in allegiance when, on surrendering, he suddenly praises Lord Fairfax in terms that he never uses for King Charles—as a hero comparable to Gustavus Adolphus (pp. 301–02). He reports with admiration Lord Fairfax's hope that King Charles would "settle the Kingdom in Peace, that *Englishmen* might not wound and destroy one another" (p. 301).

As the Cavalier points out, such praise of Lord Fairfax comes from someone unsympathetic to the Parliament's cause and from a soldier who had fought bravely for the King as long as fighting was possible. This makes him into a generous and impartial admirer. His biases are clear, and by the end of the work, we are familiar with his pattern of thought. If the ideal historian is an impartial spectator, then the Cavalier hardly fits the pattern; but if, as La Mothe le Vayer claimed, bias is inevitable in a historian,[47] then the Cavalier at least clarifies his prejudices in such a way as to be the ideal writer of memoirs. We may not know much about the Cavalier's love life and may wonder about his visit to Bath with two ladies to whom he is related—a visit that results in his missing an important battle. But we know all that is necessary to understand his attitudes toward the great political and military events of his century.

III

If the particular narrative shape of *Memoirs of a Cavalier* is essentially fictional in treatment of structure, character, and the flow of experience, it is equally true of *A Journal of the Plague Year*. Sir Walter Scott attempted to explain the reader's fascination with Defoe's account of the plague by appealing to his ability at evoking a sense of reality. "The subject is hideous almost to disgust," wrote Scott, "yet . . . like Pistol eating his leek, we go on growling and reading to the end of the volume, while we nod over many a more elegant subject."[48] Scott's criticism, including the suggestion that the realism was merely a kind of trick, has guided much of the critical commentary that followed, but modern critics have split on the relation of fiction to history in the work. One has argued that the Saddler is Defoe's uncle, Henry Foe, rendered biographically, and that, whenever possible, Defoe aimed at accurate historical presentation. Another has maintained that H. F. is a complex fictional character to whose inner experiences or "meditations" we owe our experience of the novel.[49] Even more radical than the suggestions that we examine the work as either history or a psychological novel is John Robert Moore's brief comment that the book was intended as a defense of the Quarantine Act of 1721;[50] the government's plan to isolate London from the rest of the nation should the plague, then raging in Southern France, reach the city. The reason I find this radical is that it would force us to think of the book as government propaganda directed at England in 1722 rather than as history or historical fiction about 1665. But as we have seen in Defoe's defense of European Protestantism and English Dissent in *Memoirs of a Cavalier*, he could have it both ways.

To garner some idea of what London was like during the plague, who is so useful as Samuel Pepys? The diarist shows some distress throughout his stay in London, yet after remarking that "the likelihood of the increase of the plague this week makes us a little sad," he immediately adds, "But then again, the thoughts of the late prizes [in the war] makes us glad." And in his last entry for 1665, he summarizes his sense of the year's events in a burst of good feeling: "I have never lived so merrily (besides that I never got so much) as I have done this plague-time, by my Lord Brouncker's and Captain Cocke's good company, and the acquaintance of Mrs. Knipp, Coleman and her husband, and Mr. Laneare; and a great store of dancings we have had at my cost (which I willing to indulge myself and my wife) at my lodgings."[51] Pepys is slightly inconvenienced and sometimes a little frightened. Like H. F., the Saddler, he is fascinated by the spectacle of death, but for the most part, his concerns focus on the war with the Dutch, on his efforts at bringing together the shy couple, Philip Carteret and Jemima Montagu, and on his pursuit of various ladies.

Pepys' *Diary* gives the satisfying feeling of the continuity of ordinary life and experience during a disaster and tells us just how odd the *Journal of the Plague Year* is. Neither the life of the time nor even the life of the plague occurred in quite the way Defoe presented it. The historian of the plague of 1665, Walter G. Bell, warned his readers that Defoe's book had to be read as a "historical novel," however vivid and accurate individual details might be.[52] For one thing, Defoe gives us the sense of an entire city population struggling with the plague, though at the time it was called "the Poors Plague" in recognition of the class that made up most of the victims. As Professor Louis Landa has remarked in his introduction to his excellent edition of *A Journal of the Plague Year*, the book is "first and foremost a story of London. . . . Where deaths are so abundant, poignancy is diffused. The real tragedy is corporate."[53] Rich and poor, Professor Landa states, died together. But no magistrate died in the real London of 1665, and Defoe, who knew his London so well, must have known where and whom the plague attacked. His H. F. is surely the first fictional narrator whose sympathies embrace the swarming poor of the city.

Bell also complained that Defoe had structured his fiction around the false notion that an efficient London administration had maintained order and supplied bread throughout the plague just as in the city of Leipzig during the terrible siege of the Thirty Years War. There had actually been much disorder, and in his rewrite of Defoe's books on the plague into the historical romance *Old St. Pauls*, William Harrison Ainsworth, probably thinking that Defoe had missed a good fictional opportunity, wrote in numerous scenes of disorder and added a whole cast of villains.[54] There are no villains in Defoe's rewriting of the past, with the possible exception of a few atheistical scoffers, and his reason for suggesting that the magistrates maintained order was not to support the Quarantine Act, as Moore thought, but rather to suggest that for the English constitution, a small amount of chaos was more acceptable than a lessening of freedom. The Saddler is sympathetic toward the poor in discussing the possibility of an insurrection during the height of the epidemic, arguing that they were "starv'd for want of Work, and by that means for want of Bread." Only a Malthusian solution prevents the revolt:

This, I say, was only a Rumour, and it was very well it was no more; but it was not so far off from being a Reality, as it had been thought, for in a few Weeks more the poor People became so Desperate by the Calamity they suffer'd, that they were with great difficulty kept from running out into the Fields and Towns, and tearing all in pieces where-ever they came; and, as I have observed before, nothing hinder'd them but that the

Plague rag'd so violently, and fell in upon them so furiously, that they rather went to the Grave by Thousands than into the Fields in Mobs by Thousands: For . . . where the Mob began to threaten, the Distemper came on so furiously, that there died in those few Parishes, even then, before the Plague was come to its height, no less than 5361 People in the first three Weeks in August. [Pp. 128–29]

But so far from praising the idea of closing houses and quarantining the city, Defoe's narrator presents as a "Pattern for all poor Men to follow, or Women either, if ever such a Time comes again" (p. 122): the march of three poor craftsmen through London and into the countryside in defiance of all measures to prevent them. And in one news report of the plague in France, he presents a vivid picture of how soldiers killed 178 people, including thirty women and children, attempting to flee Toulon, and still failed to prevent some from breaking through the lines. Although London's magistrates petitioned for a repeal of the Quarantine Act, only a few Jacobites and Tories supported them in Parliament until, finally, Walpole indicated by his silence that he would not object to the repeal. A loyal Londoner, Defoe was not ready to see his city cut off from the rest of the country and left to die.

Now in a proper context, the passage from the *Journal of the Plague Year* that I quoted dealing with the threat of an insurrection might have had a place in a genuine history of the plague, but it is clear that this kind of combination of narrative and analysis is not where the real energy of Defoe's fictional account lies. When we read a straight narrative chronicle of the plague of 1665 in Nathaniel Hodges's *Loimologia*, we recognize how different Defoe's work is; only when Hodges moves from narrative of events to his individual medical cases do we recognize some of the effects achieved by Defoe.[55] Narrative does not function in *A Journal of the Plague Year* as a mode of "historical explanation"; to the contrary, it is history that functions as a subsidiary organizational device for various fictions in the narrative.[56]

Borges has remarked: "There is no point in being overwhelmed by the appalling total of human suffering; such a total does not exist. Neither poverty nor pain is accumulable."[57] In fact, Defoe does not give us much of the panorama of mass suffering, just enough to let us know it exists. H. F. tells us:

It is impossible to describe the most horrible Cries and Noise the poor People would make at their bringing the dead Bodies of their Children and Friends out to the Cart, and by the Number one would have thought, there had been none left behind, or that there were People enough for a small City liveing in those Places: Several times they cryed Murther, sometimes Fire; but it was easie to perceive it was all Distraction, and the Complaints of Distress'd and distemper'd People. [P. 178]

But Defoe avoids metaphors, like the Dance of Death, which abound in Dekker's accounts of the plague[58] and which Ainsworth found so irresistible that he built that particular one into a major scene.[59] Stock images produce stock responses: what Defoe wanted was the individual agony in the individual story—the tale of the man who dies beside his sick wife "sunk under the weight of his Grief" (p. 120), or the horror of the woman suddenly kissed by one of the plague victims while walking in the street. Such moments are best described by Frank Kermode's term for novelistic time, *kairos,* "a point in time filled with significance, charged with a meaning derived from its relation to the end."[60] Such moments in the novel operate against *chronos,* the passing time of history.

If passages of this kind remove the reader from the flow of history, they also divert the reader from any focus on the narrator. H. F. witnesses these moments, but they are his moments only in some remote phenomenological sense. When the Saddler meets Robert, the Waterman who continues working during the plague in order to support his sick wife and children, he tells us how deeply moved he is by the spectacle of simple, honest devotion to family, but our focus is on Robert not on the narrator. The novel ends with the triumphant survival of the Saddler, but whereas in *Robinson Crusoe* we hardly think of all those men who died when Crusoe was saved, our real joy in *A Journal of the Plague Year* is for the survival of London and the core of her people—the poor who remained. And since his focus was different, Defoe did not need as dramatized a narrator as in *Memoirs of a Cavalier.*

IV

In concluding, I would like to draw together what I have said about the function of history in Defoe's work and make a few observations on the relationship between fictional narratives and historical narratives. It seems to me that, despite the lack of a romantic plot in either *Memoirs of a Cavalier* or *A Journal of the Plague Year* and the lack in the latter of what Georg Lukács has called a "world historical individual,"[61] both works have to be read as historical novels rather than as history manqué. Some of the objections to this classification date from nineteenth-century preconceptions of what a novel ought to be. For example, one critic, writing on Ainsworth, preferred *Old St. Pauls* to Defoe's study of the plague because it was "peopled" with characters. Modern readers have to find Ainsworth's use of quaint figures like Solomon Eagle an embarrassment. If we think of the historical novel as being essentially a play of costumes in which a variety of historical figures act out romantic roles, Defoe was writing something else, but if we conceive of it, ideally, as a type of fiction having a dynamic concept of history functioning for both the past and the present, then Defoe's two novels qualify better than Ainsworth's *Old St. Pauls.* Certainly the renewed interest in Sir Walter Scott's fiction has more to do with what he had to say about the relationship of human beings to historical events than with any revival of admiration for his heroes and heroines.[62]

Defoe's Cavalier is a participant in events in a way that the Saddler is not and takes on a specificity of character that the Saddler lacks. But both men are at the service of events. Even Gustavus Adolphus seems to win at the Battle of Lech only because a stray bullet happens to kill Tilly, the general of the Imperialists; and the battles of Edgehill and Marston Moor are won and lost by forces that seem beyond any rational human control. The heroic "Captain" John, the biscuit baker who leads his friends out of London and into the countryside, beyond the dangers of the plague, is typical of the kind of hero produced by particular events. After the plague, he will probably go back to his trade, but momentarily at least he is an important figure. Defoe never forgot that history was something that happened to masses of people, not just to Kings and Queens.

I have argued elsewhere that throughout the *Journal of the Plague Year* there is a gradual identification of the "people" with the suffering masses and a tendency toward reconciliation.[63] The two are connected insofar as great disasters not only reconcile men of various beliefs, as happens in *Memoirs of a Cavalier*, but also tend to reduce the barriers of social distinction. The history that Defoe uses as the background for his two historical novels has something of the quality that Gerhard von Rad found in the "saga" of a people, a work binding the present to the past and renewing the contractual relationship of the individual to his society through a narrative recounting the victories of his ancestor over adversity: "a view and interpretation not only of that which once was but of a past event that is secretly present and decisive for the present."[64] Behind the resignation of the Cavalier in 1645 and the Saddler's triumph over the terror of 1665 lay a fictional patterning of history and a message for the chaos of his own time and, perhaps, for all times.

W. B. Gallie has warned historians: "Let the critical, doubting, questioning, assessing attitude of mind lapse—or rise—into the sheer joy of following an absorbing narrative, and the historical mind has passed into the land of story, and is heading hard towards the land of dreams."[65] But the land of dreams is obviously central to the concerns of fictional narrative. The theoretical connections between history and the novel are alluring, particularly to modern historians, but for the literary critic they are likely to lead to conclusions that are almost self-evident—that writers of fiction, even historical fiction, have more play for invention than historians.[66] With a writer like Defoe, whose mind gravitated toward fiction, we have to be more concerned with the continual presence of fiction in his nonfictional writings than the other way around. Distinguishing between the poet and the philosopher, Vico noted that the poet "works, as it were, with 'invented' examples. As a result, he may depart from the daily semblances of truth, in order to be able to frame a loftier semblance of reality. He departs from inconstant, unpredictable nature in order to pursue a more constant, more abiding reality. He creates imaginary figments which, in a way, are more real than physical reality itself."[67] As much as he admired history, as much as he learned from its rhetoric and sense of evidence, Defoe never forgot that more might be achieved through the inventive powers of the artist.

4
"Unweary'd Traveller" and
"Indifferent Monitor":
Openness and Complexity
in *Moll Flanders*

Newgate thy dwelling was, thy beauty made thee
A goddess seem, and that alone betray'd thee.
Twelve years a whore, a wife unto thy brother,
And such a thief there scarce could be another.
Unweary'd traveller, whither dost thou roam?
Lo! in this place remote to find a tomb
Transported hence, to heaven, 'tis hop'd
thou'rt sent
Who wicked liv'd, but dy'd a penitent.
(POEM APPENDED TO A CHAPBOOK VERSION OF
Moll Flanders.)[1]

IN *Lavengro*, George Borrow tells of his encounter with an old woman who kept a fruit stall on a London Bridge. He notices that she is reading a book "intently" and then finds himself grasped by her as he leans over the edge to see a boat caught in the swift-moving waters. She has been watching him and concluded that he was a pickpocket down on his luck who decided to put an end to his life. He enters into conversation with her and discovers that she has a son at Botany Bay as a transported felon and that she sees no harm in stealing. In fact, she offers to act as a fence for any handkerchiefs he might have taken that day. Her views on theft are conditioned by her continued love for her thieving son who certainly would not do anything wrong and by her admiration for the heroine of the book she reads so eagerly—Moll Flanders. To the author's question about the "harm" in theft, she responds:

'No harm in the world, dear! Do you think my own child would have been transported, if there had been any harm in it? and what's more, would the blessed woman in the book here have written her life as she has done, and given it to the world, if there had been any harm in faking? She, too, was what they call a thief and a cutpurse; ay, and was transported for it, like my dear son; and do you think she would have told the world so, if there had been any harm in the thing? Oh, it is a comfort to me that the blessed woman was transported, and came back— for come back she did, and rich too—for it is an assurance to me that my dear son, who was transported too, will come back like her.'

'What was her name?'

'Her name, blessed Mary Flanders.'[2]

Borrow, who has told his readers how he learned to read by his fascination with *Robinson Crusoe*, offers to buy the book from her as soon as he discovers in it "the air, the style, the spirit" of Defoe, but she refuses to sell it. "Without my book," she tells him, "I should mope and pine, and perhaps fling myself into the river." Instead, for six pence, she allows him to read it whenever he comes by. After some "wicked boys" try to steal the book from her, the old fruit seller loses some of her enthusiasm for the work, but the one time that Borrow, or his autobiographical hero, takes advantage of the chance to read, he finds himself so engrossed in it that hours pass by without his taking his eyes off the pages before him.

Now Borrow is engaging in some mythmaking of his own in creating the old fruit seller, who lives courageously on her slender earnings. Not surprisingly, it is the mythical Moll Flanders who is perceived by the old woman. She knows nothing about the warnings against stealing that Borrow points out to her. She reads it as a fairy tale, noticing only the "funny parts" and reaping from it a fund of hope that keeps her optimistic in spite of the grim facts of her life. Only when she begins to lose hope, which occurs after the attempted theft of the book, does she turn from it and agree to the author's offer to buy her a Bible in its place.[3]

From some standpoints the old fruit woman is a bad reader, but what she perceives in *Moll Flanders* is certainly present in Defoe's work. This is the Moll who will not allow her difficulties to plunge her into despair, who rises above her situation to become a success—a successful servant, mistress, wife, thief, whore, plantation owner, and mother. Whatever warnings he wanted to give to thieves, he was more intent on telling them that they could find new lives in a New World. And Defoe knew that his audience tended to find a kind of subversive heroism in the new breed of thief and pirate that emerged at the start of the eighteenth century.[4] Defoe excused many of Moll's acts on the grounds of poverty and necessity and, up to a point, gave the audience what they wanted.

I

Borrow does not tell us what edition of *Moll Flanders* it is that the old woman reads over and over again. If it was long enough to occupy Borrow for a number of hours, it was not one of the brief chapbook versions produced toward the end of the eighteenth century, but it may not have been Defoe's original work for all of that. Yet *Moll Flanders* received even briefer treatment in the ballad versions. The one that follows even deletes part of Defoe's title:

The Misfortunes of Moll Flanders

MOLL Flanders born in Newgate by man it is said.
Her tricks & fine manners I mean for to display
Seventeen times she was a lewd woman 5 times she was
a wife,
And a slave to Virginia she was condemned for life.

For fam'd Shoplifting she surely bore the belle
For beauty & for artfulness none could her excell
To her own brother once was marry'd, dreadful tale
to tell,
At Hounslow, and at Finchley, did often cut a swell.

The pitcher so often to the well it came home, broke at
last.
Moll Flanders famous husband at length was try'd and cast,
The facts against him were so plain and awful did appear.
He at Tyburn suffer'd death for this crime as we hear.

A slave at Virginia she handled the Hoe,
Amongst West Indian Negroes she suffered many a blow,
An Eye witness to the cruelties that was inflicted there
She wish'd herself at home again upon her native shore.

But Providence that reigns above on her cast an eye,
Her mistress shewed her favour shed many a bitter sigh,
Though her misfortunes they were great she proved fortunate
at last
Lived honest and dy'd penitent lament her follies past.

Such an extraordinary character you never heard before.
And so you will say I know full well when this book
you do read o'er,
No one would scarcely credit what she did undergo.
Be warn'd by her you young and gay & honestly pursue.[5]

Defoe obviously had nothing to do with this piece of doggerel, but it is useful to see what remains of his novel. She is still the child born in Newgate, still the great beauty as well as the great sinner, and still the success in the end. But except for her sex and the incestuous marriage to her brother, most of the events fit the life of Colonel Jack better than they do Moll's. Defoe's Moll is different. Moll's husband is not hanged, she never handles a hoe or has to labor in America, and she is not rescued from life among the slaves by her "mistress." One might well wonder if this was the ballad that inspired Hogarth's Idle Apprentice to commit his crimes.

Defoe's *Moll Flanders* has a brief but open ending in which she tells of her return to England and the penitence for her wicked life that the preface puts in doubt. Like most of the abridgments and chapbook versions, the ballad tries to give it more of an ending with a report of her death and a moral on her life. Borrow's old fruit seller focuses on Moll's return to England at the end as an indication that her son will return from Australia to live rich and happy in England, though most of the abridgments, if they do not have her die after a long and happy life in Virginia, bring her back to her husband's lands in Ireland where she is supposed to die after her husband and be buried in the same grave with him. The longest of the abridgments, *The History of Laetitia Atkins*, published in 1776 and ascribed to Defoe on the title page actually prints her will with its generous gifts to the servants and its assignment of most of her property to her husband's brother, William Carrol, along with an account of her pious death surrounded by "eminent divines."[6]

All of this suggests that *Moll Flanders* has a mythic life of its own. Like Betteredge, who consults *Robinson Crusoe* as a holy book that will provide him with all the answers to the problems of life, Borrow's fruit woman treats her copy of *Moll Flanders* as a magical text.[7] If Moll Flanders could steal, there could be nothing wrong with theft. When Borrow brings the old woman a Bible to replace *Moll Flanders* as the book by which the woman will guide her life, he replaces one magical text with another. The Bible, however, begins to function for her only after she recalls a dim commandment from her youth: "Thou shalt not steal." Only after she begins to worry about her life and values does she begin to tire of the subversive text by which she has been living.

Of course, Borrow's insistence that she has been misreading Defoe's work has its point too. She transforms Moll into a patron saint of criminals—"blessed Mary Flanders." She sees humor in it, but she is incapable of following the subtleties of Defoe's language, and she simply ignores Moll's direct moralizing on crime. In her own way, she edits as she reads and transforms Defoe's novel into her private rendition of the short, chapbook versions that provided little more than the myth of the clever and successful criminal. That is hardly what *Moll Flanders* is really about. I want to turn now to examine what an ideal reader might discover beyond the myth.

II

Behold the cruel Hand of death,
Hath snatch'd away Elizabeth.
Twelve Years she was an arant Whore;
Was sometimes rich, and sometimes poor;
Which made her, when she'd no Relief,
Be full as many Years a Thief.
In this Carier of Wickedness,
Poor Betty *always had success;*
(FROM A CHAPBOOK VERSION OF *Moll Flanders*)[8]

I leave the Readers of these things to their own just Reflections, which they will be more able to make effectual than I, who so soon forgot my self, and am therefore but a very indifferent Monitor. DEFOE, *The Fortunes and Misfortunes of the Famous Moll Flanders.*[9]

Among the many contemporary attacks on Daniel Defoe, one of more than usual interest, entitled *The Republican Bullies* (1705), pretended to report a dialogue between Defoe (Mr. Review) and John Tutchin, author of a journal called *The Observator*. After stating that he wants no part of sword fights, Defoe explains that he is more adept at destroying his enemies with irony:

> Rev. No man would dispute the Prize with you, if downright Billingsgate was the Weapon to gain by it. He's the Champion for a Modern Readers Mony, that can cut a Throat with a Feather, that can wound the sacred Order by way of Expostulations and fling Dirt upon them by Dint of Irony as I have done.
>
> Obs. The only Figure in Rhetorick that you are Master of! More thanks to Nature than Art, who has given it to you, without so much as letting you know that it is One.[10]

That his contemporaries recognized that his "peculiar Talent" lay in presenting effective arguments through the use of irony, satire, and fiction is obvious enough to anyone who has studied the numerous, grudging compliments given him by his enemies. His reputation as a poet and a pamphleteer declined only when his work for the government forced him into such dull repetition and absurd contradiction that even his amazing wit and intelligence had to fail him.

But whatever his contemporaries may have thought of him, two facts have become apparent from the recent critical debates over *Moll Flanders:* (1) that he may have been ironic in some of his pamphlets is no guarantee that he was being ironic in *Moll Flanders;* (2) that his contemporaries regarded his manner as ironic does not mean that what he did satisfied some modern critics' concepts of irony. Until some universally acceptable definition of irony can be established, critics will continue to disagree, and I have no intention in this chapter to revive a discussion that has proved so inconclusive.[11] Instead, I want to examine in detail some of the complexities of language and narrative in *Moll Flanders* that have led me and some other critics to doubt that they are dealing with a fiction involving a straightforward fictional confession and imagine that Moll's was the kind of ironic narrative Defoe might have inherited from picaresque fiction directly or through the influence of the picaresque on criminal biography.[12]

Some useful information about the genesis of Defoe's novel was provided in 1968 by Gerald Howson, whose article in *TLS*, "Who Was Moll Flanders?" tells us a great deal about the criminals who formed the basis for Defoe's narrator.[13] Moll Flanders, we learn, was imaginatively constructed from several women criminals of the time, particularly two known by the names Moll King and Callico Sarah. Since Defoe was visiting his friend, the publisher Mist, in Newgate at the same time these two ladies were there, he would have had numerous opportunities to converse with them. Moll King managed to survive from five to eight sentences of transportation without being hanged, and if some critics have discovered in Moll Flanders' life a mythic, symbolic sense of human endurance, they might well feel justified.

Defoe may even have taken his heroine's name from an indirect combination of the names of these two women, since *Flanders* was the name for a Flemish lace, a contraband article figuring in one of Moll Flanders' thefts. Howson allows that the contemporary advertisement for *The History of Flanders with Moll's Map*, a reference to the work of the cartographer Herman Moll, may have given Defoe his initial idea, but he advances his suggestion concerning the relation between callico and lace as being more relevant, and I agree. Now the genesis of Defoe's title may seem completely unimportant, but I want to argue that this suggestive use of language is one of the most important elements in *Moll Flanders* and a key to its complexity.

Though Defoe's lapses from consistency have often caused his artistic integrity to be called into question, he was a writer deeply concerned with language and the meaning of words—the way an understanding of subtle shifts in meaning distinguishes the good writer from the bad. Let us suppose for the moment that Defoe set out to present a character who passes over certain points of her life with evasive remarks and comes close to lying about others. How would it be possible to handle the language of narrative in such a way that something resembling a true view of the events would be apparent to the reader? Wayne Booth has pointed out the difficulties with proving ironic intent in a novel written in the first person, and Defoe was not above solving this problem in pamphlets employing a persona by ending them with a direct confession of what he called "Irony."[14] But realistic fiction would prevent a device of this kind. What Defoe needed was a method of making meaning transparent without sacrificing the integrity of his point of view.

One way out was through a complex use of language and what Defoe called "Inuendo," by which he meant all indirect methods of communication from irony to meiosis. If we turn to the point in Defoe's novel when Moll has been abandoned by the lover she picked up at Bath, some of the complications involved will be clear. After receiving a note from him cutting off the affair, Moll writes a letter telling him that she would never be able to recover from the blow of parting from him, that she not only approved of his repentance but wished "to Repent as sincerely as he had done." (p. 125) All she needs is fifty pounds to return to Virginia. Moll confesses at once that what she said "was indeed all a Cheat," and that "the business was to get this last Fifty Pounds of him," but she does moralize on the situation:

> And here I cannot but reflect upon the unhappy Consequence of too great Freedoms between Persons started as we were, upon the pretence of innocent intentions, Love of Friendship, *and the like;* for the Flesh has generally so great a share in those Friendships, that it is great odds but inclination prevails at last over the most solemn Resolutions and that Vice breaks in at the breaches of Decency, which really innocent Friendship ought to preserve with the greatest strictness; but I leave the Readers of these things to their own just Reflections, which they will be more able to make effectual than I, who so soon forgot my self, and am therefore but a very indifferent Monitor. [P. 126]

Moll's willingness to confess that any admonitions coming from her about manners and morals might well be regarded sceptically should put the reader on guard at once. Would we want to hear morality preached by Moll King or Callico Sarah? And after all, Moll has just testified to her dishonesty. Surely at this point sim-

---

Illustrations of some of Moll Flanders's adventures from an abridgment published by Thomas Read around 1723.

ple solutions (e.g., it is Defoe with his somewhat questionable puritan moral standards speaking) will not work.

There are also disturbing stylistic elements in the passage that might prevent the reader from regarding it as a straightforward confession. Take the phrase, "Love of Friendship, *and the like.*" One might also think that Moll was being witty, that *"and the like"* was intended to imply by ironic understatement all the possible kinds of discourses leading ultimately to seduction. Although Professor Watt has warned us against reading into Defoe what is not there, this is an important element in Moll's narrative.[15] She is always qualifying words in order to clarify the distinction between the apparent meaning of a word and the reality behind it. The brother she lived with in incest is "my Brother, *as I now call him*" (p. 127), the first woman who takes care of her is "my Mistress Nurse, *as I call'd her*" (p. 9), the trunk she steals from a Dutchman is "my Trunk, *as I call'd it*" (p. 265). Whether or not Defoe actually added the italics to these phrases (as he did occasionally in the one extensive manuscript of his that we have),[16] they were obviously intended to suggest the disparity between what something is called and what it is, and to call attention to the narrator's own awareness of this.[17]

Similar to these kinds of phrases is her simple remark, "I WAV'D the Discourse" when her Bank Manager sums up the character of his wife with the remark, "she that will be *a Whore* will be *a Whore,*" or her summation of her reaction to the entire tale of this sad cuckold, "Well, I pitied him, and wish'd him well rid of her, and still would have talk'd of my Business" (p. 135). The tone of impatience (the Bank Manager is married and therefore unavailable at this point) is clear enough. Defoe *is* conveying a great deal, then, through tone and language.

In fact Moll is extraordinarily playful in her use of language. When she tries to avoid joining a gang of counterfeiters, she remarks, "tho' I had declin'd it with the greatest assurances of Secresy in the World, they would have gone near to have murther'd me, to make sure Work, and make themselves easy, *as they call it;* what kind of easiness that is, they may best Judge that understand how easy Men are, that can murther People to prevent Danger" (p. 255). And the section in which she enters the home for unwed mothers is full of such implications. After the

Governess has assured her that she need not worry about the care of her child if she puts it out to a nurse recommended by the house and that she must behave as "other conscientious Mothers" (p. 176), Moll, who is careful to separate herself from "all those Women who consent to the disposing their Children out of the way, *as it is call'd*" (p. 173), comments on her Governess's language: "I understood what she meant by conscientious Mothers, she would have said conscientious Whores; but she was not willing to disoblige me" (p. 176). Moll tells herself that, at least technically, she was married, but then merely contents herself with distinguishing herself from other prostitutes ("the Profession") by her still tender heart. Even the affectionate use of the term *Mother* for her Governess is suspect. Though she might have a right to that title by her affectionate treatment of Moll, or by being Moll's "Mother Midnight" (p. 162), that is, her midwife, the name was usually given to the madam of a brothel. In fact their dialogues resemble nothing so much as those between Mother Cresswell and Dorothea, bawd and neophyte, in *The Whore's Rhetorick* (1683). They, too, refer to each other as mother and daughter, and Moll's Mother-Governess is not above being a bawd as well as an abortionist and a fence.

Perhaps the way in which Moll describes the suggestion of an abortion and her rejection of it gives the best clues to the complex use of language in Defoe's novel:

> The only thing I found in all her Conversation on these Subjects, that gave me any distaste, was, that one time in Discoursing about my being so far gone with Child, and the time I expected to come, she said something that look'd as if she could help me off with my Burthen sooner, if I was willing; or in *English,* that she could give me something to make me Miscarry, if I had a desire to put an end to my Troubles that way; but I soon let her see that I abhorr'd the Thoughts of it; and to do her Justice, she put it off so cleverly, that I could not say she really intended it, or whether she only mentioned the practice as a horrible thing; for she couch'd her words so well, and took my meaning so quickly, that she gave her Negative before I could explain myself. [Pp. 168–69]

Moll used the same pun a few pages before (p. 161); if the reader failed to catch it the first time, he might be at least as clever as Moll's Governess and pick it up the second time around. One can assume, then, that, at times, Moll converses in double-entendres and expects her listeners and readers to understand them.[18]

Such word play is not uncommon in Defoe's narrative. As I have indicated elsewhere,[19] Moll points to her misunderstanding of the use of the word *Miss* by the wife of the mayor who comes to visit her when she is a child in Colchester: "The Word Miss was a Language that had hardly been heard of in our School, and I wondered what sad Name it was she call'd me" (p. 8). It is a sad word because it says something about her future quest after gentility and her future life as a prostitute. In much the same way, thinking of the friend who has passed her off as a woman of fortune, Moll tells of how she decides to take a trip to Bath. "I took the Diversion of going to the *Bath*," she remarks, "for as I was still far from being old, so my Humour, which was always Gay, continu'd so to an Extream; and being now, *as it were*, a Woman of Fortune, tho' I was a Woman without a Fortune, I expected something, or other might happen in my way, that might mend my Circumstances, as had been my Case before" (p. 106). Another instance of this type of word play comes in the section on the counterfeiters. Speaking of her refusal to join the gang, Moll remarks that

the part they would have had me have embark'd in, was the most dangerous Part; I mean that of the very working the Dye, as they call it, which had I been taken, had been certain Death, and that at a Stake, *I say*, to be burnt to Death at a Stake; so that tho' I was to Appearance, but a Beggar; and they promis'd Mountains of Gold and Silver to me, to engage; yet it would not do; it is True, if I had been really a Beggar, or had been desperate as when I began, I might perhaps have clos'd with it, for what care they to Die, that can't tell how to Live? [Pp. 254–55]

The phrase, "working the Dye," which James Sutherland calls a "grim pun" in his edition of *Moll Flanders*, meant to stamp the coin.[20] A terrible death awaits those who would gamble or stake their lives on such an occupation, and in the midst of her punning, Moll is careful to remark that "they" use the term "working the Dye," not she. This is her way of separating herself from such awful people.

It is passages like these that lead the reader to suspect other double meanings. When Moll is made pregnant by her Bath

Lover, he assumes the name of Sir Walter Cleave, and Moll says that she was made as comfortable as she would have been had she "really been my Lady *Cleave*" (p. 117). In addition to whatever sexual significance might be attached to this word by a wary reader, a "cleave" is defined as "a forward or wanton woman" in Francis Grose's *A Classical Dictionary of the Vulgar Tongue*. And significantly enough, in the rather pious chapbook versions of Moll Flanders, the name was changed to Clare.[21]

At other times the issue is doubtful. Is Moll aware of any sexual significance in a phrase like that already quoted in Moll's reflections on her Bath Lover, that "Vice breaks in at the breaches of Decency" (p. 152)? If we regard Moll as being, at least in part, a comic figure, we would have to say that Defoe makes her use this phrase with some ambiguity. Is she supposed to understand certain implications in such language? Did Defoe? Having no definite solution, I will follow Moll and waive the discourse. But of Defoe's use of puns and word play as a method to convey subtle meanings playing underneath Moll's narrative there cannot be the slightest doubt.

III

If some passages raise doubts in the reader's mind, there is good reason for it: Moll, herself, is often undecided or uncertain about the way she should interpret the events of her life, and her language often reflects these doubts. She begins the story of her Bath lover's control over his sexual desires with a remark that reveals her undecided state. He has spent the night in bed with her entirely naked and without offering any advances that might be regarded as completely sexual in nature. Moll comments, "I OWN it was a noble Principle, but as it was what I never understood before, so it was to me perfectly amazing" (p. 115). Even if one understands by "noble Principle" something that cannot work in practice, we cannot come to such a decision until Moll's final condemnation of the entire relationship several pages later.

Such passages are complex not so much because of the language alone but because Defoe asks us to suspend our judgment on the meaning of certain words and phrases until the events themselves or Moll's last commentary clarifies the situation.

Many of Moll's comments on her Governess are rich in this kind of momentary ambiguity. When the woman chosen by the Governess to tutor Moll in the art of thievery has been taken and sentenced to death, the emotions of the Governess have to be ambiguous, since the tutoress has enough information to save her own life by impeaching the Governess. Moll King saved her life several times in this manner. Moll Flanders does not render such a mixture of regret for the loss of a friend and apprehension for personal safety in anything resembling straight description:

> It is true, that when she was gone, and had not open'd her Mouth to tell what she knew; my Governess was easy as to that Point, and perhaps glad she was hang'd; for it was in her power to have obtain'd a Pardon at the Expence of her Friends; But on the other Hand, the loss of her, and the Sense of her Kindness in not making her Market of what she knew, mov'd my Governess to Mourn very sincerely for her: I comforted her as well as I cou'd, and she in return harden'd me to Merit more compleatly the same Fate. [P. 208]

Moll's bitterness is apparent enough, but the language is sometimes pointed, sometimes neutral in a situation that is inherently ambiguous. The Governess, whose life has been spared at this point and later threatened in the same way by Moll's capture, is sincere in her sorrow, but she does not undergo any change of heart. And Moll may be speaking of one point in the past, but she has her mind set on another point—her future sufferings in Newgate.

I will speak more fully of the problems of time in Moll's narrative later in this chapter, but it should be noted here that in passages such as these, Moll's narrative may be viewed ironically (by anyone's definition) on the present level of the told narrative, while functioning realistically as a record of the action as it is occurring. Many of the contradictions that appear in the novel are caused by the simple fact that even criminals and fences have to have a morality to live by. Polls among jail inmates revealing strong moral disapproval of crime are commonplace. As we shall see, such moral judgments need not indicate a permanent change of heart.

When Moll commits her "second Sally into the World" (p. 194), she tells of her experience in a manner that is even more demanding of complex understanding. Having led the little girl out of her way, Moll is confronted by the child's protests. She quiets these objections with the sinister remark, "I'll show you the way home" (p. 194). This piece of direct dialogue is given in a narrative scene to underscore its ironic implication—the possibility that to quiet the child while she was stealing the necklace she might have to murder her. After describing her horror at the impulse to murder, Moll tells of her psychological state after this robbery. "The last Affair," she says, "left no great Concern upon me" (p. 194), explaining that after all she did not harm the child and may have helped improve the care that the parents of the child would show in the future. And after estimating the value of the string of beads, Moll begins to extrapolate about the entire incident. The girl was wearing the necklace because the mother was proud; the child was being neglected by the mother, who had put her in the care of a maid; the maid was doubtless negligent and meeting her lover. And while all these palliations for her crime are being offered—and they sound peculiarly like crimes Moll might have been guilty of at other stages of her career—the "pretty little Child" has gradually become the "poor Child," "poor Lamb," and "poor Baby." In blaming everyone else but herself, Moll is revealing that her psychological involvement is far greater than she is willing to admit, and the energy that she exerts to deny her involvement is undercut verbally by the increasing sympathy she tries to arouse for the child.

As for blaming such moralizing on Defoe's simplemindedness, it should be pointed out that a later incident shows a similar unwillingness to accept guilt mingled with a more obvious callousness toward crime. When Moll seduces a Gentleman in a coach, she moralizes on the possibility that the man might have been seduced by a diseased prostitute. Her moralizing, it should be noted, is a blend of past and present reactions:

As for me, my Business was his Money, and what I could make of him, and after that if I could have found out any way to have done it, I would have sent him safe home to his House, and to his Family, for 'twas ten to one but he had an honest virtuous Wife, and innocent Children, that were anxious for his Safety, and would have been glad to have gotten him Home, and have taken care of him, till he was restor'd to himself; and then with what Shame and Regret would he look back upon himself?

how would he reproach himself with associating himself with a Whore? pick'd up in the worst of all Holes, the Cloister, among the Dirt and Filth of the Town? how would he be trembling for fear he had got the Pox, for fear a Dart had struck through his Liver, and hate himself every time he look'd back upon the Madness and Brutality of his Debauch? how would he, if he had any Principles of Honour, as I verily believe he had, I say how would he abhor the Thought of giving any ill Distemper, if he had it, as for ought he knew he might, to his Modest and Virtuous Wife, and thereby sowing the Contagion in the Life-Blood of his Posterity? [P. 227]

What is curious about this is that Moll is substantially creating a fiction as she goes along in much the same manner as she did with the child she robbed. The fiction about the gentleman led astray by the prostitute is highly moral and has little or none of the word play that, as I have shown, is a customary part of Moll's narrative manner. But it is a fiction for all that, a story woven to cheer herself up in the past and present, and the more graphic it is, the more real it is for her.

And then Moll does something that we ought to expect. She betrays herself by telling a somewhat off-color story of how, by replacing his purse with one filled with tokens during sexual intercourse, a prostitute once managed to pick the pocket of a customer, even though he was on his guard. Doubtless she tells the sad story of the gentleman who might have picked up a diseased prostitute to her Governess in as moving terms as she tells it to the reader, for she described how that good lady "was hardly able to forbear Tears, to think how such a Gentleman run a daily Risque of being undone, every Time a Glass of Wine got into his Head." But the Governess is entirely pleased by the booty Moll has brought her from the gentleman, and after assuring Moll that the incident might "do more to reform him, than all the Sermons that ever he will hear in his life" (p. 228), she proceeds to arrange a liaison between Moll and the gentleman. It is impossible to think that Defoe was napping here. Moll and her Governess possess a great deal of morality, but they are criminals nevertheless, and Defoe never lets us forget it. Moll remains throughout the novel an "indifferent Monitor."

IV

During this discussion of the complexities of language and style in *Moll Flanders*, I have touched on the intricate temporal relationships in individual passages; now I want to turn to the larger issue of time in Defoe's narrative as a further example of Defoe's considerable skill. Most modern discussions of narrative technique in *Moll Flanders* begin with a version of the concept of the "double focus" suggested by Mendilow in his *Time and the Novel*. Mendilow suggested that both *Moll Flanders* and *Roxana* belonged to that type of novel in which, because the narrator is speaking of her youth, "one often senses the gap between the action and its record." Mendilow then remarked that "two characters are superimposed one upon the other, and the impression of the one who acts is coloured and distorted by the interpretations of the one who narrates," and that the "diaries" of Moll and Roxana as they would have been written in their youth would have been far different from these retrospective narratives. Some critics have disagreed with Mendilow's conclusions, but that is probably because they failed to remark that he adds later on that novels often "contain different degrees of pastness."[22]

Certainly *Moll Flanders* is extraordinarily varied in treating levels of time, and a good example of the way we experience Moll's movement between such levels may be seen in the passages preceding the death of her Bank Manager husband. The basic technique is that of summary, but as she carries us breathlessly through the five years of happiness she had with him, she also supplies us with a vivid picture of her psychological state:

I LIV'D with this Husband in the utmost Tranquility; he was a Quiet, Sensible, Sober Man, Virtuous, Modest, Sincere, and in his Business Diligent and Just: His Business was in a narrow Compass, and his Income sufficient to a plentiful way of Living in the ordinary way; I do not say to keep an Equipage, and make a Figure as the World calls it, nor did I expect it, or desire it; for as I abhorr'd the Levity and Extravagance of my former Life, so I chose now to live retir'd, frugal, and within our selves; I kept no Company, made no Visits; minded my Family, and oblig'd my Husband; and this kind of Life became a Pleasure to me. [Pp. 188–89]

Such a passage is intended to show Moll's temporary conversion to the ideals of a middle-class marriage. But it also dips vividly into past experience. Unlike Moll's first lover, who carried her off in the coach of Sir W—— H——, her Gentleman Tradesman husband, who insisted in travelling in a *"Coach and Six,"* and her Lancashire Husband, Jemmy, who calls for her with his "Chariot . . . , with two Footmen in a good Livery" (p. 142), this husband offers her only the kind of comfort that she had always rejected. In this marriage she has rejected the "World" of fashion, which had been her envy from childhood, to find pleasure in what was Defoe's ideal—the private life of a contented family.[23]

Defoe had stated such an ideal before, but nowhere so thoroughly as in his *Condoling Letter to the Tatler* (1710), in which he portrayed human happiness as a means illustrated by a thermometer of the human condition:

> *Madness,*
> *Poverty,*
> *Extravagence,*
> *Excess or Profusion,*
> *Waste,*
> *Generous Liberality,*
> *Plenty*
> FAMILY
> *Frugality,*
> *Parsimony,*
> *Niggardliness,*
> *Covetousness,*
> *Sordidly Covetous,*
> *Wretchedness or Rich Poverty*
> *Madness*

Here is the Word FAMILY in the Centre, which signifies the Man, let his Circumstances be what it will, for every Man is a Family to himself. He is plac'd between *Plenty* and *Frugality;* a Blessed, Happy Medium, which makes Men beloved of all, respectd of the Rich, blessed by the Poor, useful to themselves, to their Country, and to their Posterity.[24]

In Defoe's thermometer of well-being, madness through wealth or poverty stands at both the bottom and the top. Moll has truly achieved a state that she comes to recognize as ideal, even if it is not what she would want if she had her choice. She is soon close to a state of desperate poverty.

Those who have seen this as the psychological and structural middle of the novel can find justification both in Moll's moral career from this point on and in the narrative. For after this summary of her present condition, which is in itself so full of echoes of the past, Moll tells of her husband's bankruptcy in terms that move forward from the way the event "turn'd . . . [her] out into the World in a Condition the reverse of all that had been before it" (p. 231), goes back in time to narrate the cause of his troubles, and tells the reader the advice she gave him. One paragraph tells of his death in a manner that skillfully reverses the event and her forebodings: "It was in vain to speak comfortably to him, the Wound had sunk too deep, it was a Stab that touch'd the Vitals, he grew Melancholy and from thence Lethargick, and died; I foresaw the Blow, and was extremely oppress'd in my Mind, for I saw evidently that if he died I was undone" (p. 189). One of the remarkable things about Defoe's style in such passages is the way he can be both concise and repetitious at the same time, a technique that Lévi-Strauss has found to be the essential narrative quality of myth.[25] Thus, when she recognizes her Lancashire Husband riding into the Inn where she is staying with her new husband, the Bank Manager, she says, "I knew his Cloaths, I knew his Horse, and I knew his Face" (p. 185). Nothing could be more dramatic and, without dwelling on her psychological state, tell us how she feels by what appears to be an external description. A similar process is at work in her account of the death of the Bank Manager. Moll is not merely telling the reader about the progress of his disease, she is explaining how she watched his decline with terror.

Much of this may be viewed as a question of style, but the important point is that Defoe was continually manipulating style to achieve narrative effects. He even changes tenses or makes use of contemporary grammatical forms that could stand for either present or past to attain a sense of immediacy in scenes of action. When a fire breaks out in the neighborhood of her Governess, Moll rushes to the scene to pick up what booty she can find:

Away I went, and coming to the House I found them all in Confusion, you may be sure; I run in, and finding one of the Maids, Lord! Sweetheart, *said I*, how came this dismal Accident? Where is your Mistress? And how does she do? Is she safe? And where are the Children? I come from Madam———to help you; away runs the Maid, Madam, madam, *says she*, screaming as loud as she cou'd yell, *here is a Gentlewoman come from Madam———to help us:* The poor Woman half out of her Wits, with a Bundle under her Arm, and two little Children, comes towards me, *Lord*

Madam, says I, let me carry the poor Children to Madam———, she desires you to send them; she'll take care of the poor Lambs, and immediately I takes one of them out of her Hand, and she lifts the other up into my arms; *ay, do for God sake,* says she . . . and away she runs from out of her Wits, and the Maids after her, and away comes I with the two Children and the Bundle. [P. 205]

Some curiosities in Defoe's grammar have led older critics to comment on his homely style, but here Defoe is taking advantage either of what would be Moll's ungrammatical manner or simply sacrificing grammar to achieve a sense of hurry and excitement. Both seem to be present in the "away she runs . . . and away comes I" section so typical of Moll in her lighter moments.

In such a passage, of course, the use of dialogue is equally important for giving the feeling of action recreated in the present. If Defoe did not succeed in getting the kind of immediacy achieved by Richardson's technique of "writing to the present," he nevertheless attempted various methods of attaining a similar effect when he needed it. *Moll Flanders* differs from Defoe's two historical novels, *Memoirs of a Cavalier* and *A Journal of the Plague Year.* As I have attempted to show, both of these function in a specific historical time, although that time is made so dramatically cogent for the present as to make it serve a purpose similar to that of fulfilled vision or prophecy. And *Moll Flanders* is also different from *Roxana,* which, as we shall see, completely distorts historical time. Yet the seeming error in having Roxana's career function in both the era of the Restoration and the eighteenth century is certainly understandable, for Defoe wanted to contrast the dissolute court of Charles II with the luxury of his own time. If his transition from one period to the other would have to be achieved by a process that is opposed to any concept of realistic chronology, it was, nevertheless, an experiment that might have been worth trying.[26]

Mendilow's formula, then, is good as far as it goes, but Defoe's world is always synchronic rather than diachronic. The past is imported into the present as a psychologically recreatable state. Hence Moll's reactions are indeed confused and ambiguous. Crusoe does not have the same difficulty separating his past from his present, and Roxana may vary between irony and passion in commenting on her past, but she is seldom without some kind of commentary. Moll's reaction to her past is somewhat reminiscent of the first person narrative of a shaman among the Kwakiutls that Franz Boas recorded. The Narrator, QāsElīd, begins as a skeptic. "Then it occurred to me," he states, "that I was the principal one who does not believe in all the ways of the shamans, for I had said so aloud to them. Now I had an opportunity by what they said that I should really learn whether they were real or whether they only pretended to be shamans."[27] Eventually, after becoming a shaman himself, he finds that the cures he works are superior to those of other shamans and comes to believe that somehow he does have curative powers. The narrative reveals a development, yet were he to begin again, he would unquestionably start with his initial scepticism and the lying and fakery among shamans. Like QāsElīd, Moll responds dynamically and ambiguously to her own narrative, reliving her past life for the reader as she recreates it for herself in the present.

This is why her conversion to Christianity, which most students find questionable, is without much of the wit and complexity to be found in most sections of the novel. If we find that her life after conversion is not what we would expect of a good Christian, we share a feeling that the "editor" informs us may have considerable basis in fact. Perhaps Moll's concern and the reader's are too strong at these moments to allow for a definition of *Moll Flanders* as an ironic novel. Certainly it does not deserve such a name if that genre is to be limited to works like Fielding's *Jonathan Wild* or Ford's *The Good Soldier*. But Defoe has Moll relive her life, responding to the emotions of the moment as they reflect her previous emotions and experiences. And if she can be both the ideal convert and the wayward servant-whore-thief at the same time, she shares with the Kwakiutl shaman the natural ability to exist in a number of states simultaneously.

My comparison of QāsElīd and Moll might lead one to the conclusion that the actual thrust of Defoe's fiction was toward a simple mirroring of reality and real personality, though, as I have tried to demonstrate throughout, fictional reality is never simple. In fact, such an argument has been advanced by Ralph Rader, who discusses Moll and her narrative as a story of the "pseudofactual type," one in which Defoe, as author, has disappeared to the extent that any judgment about the moral meaning of the

94

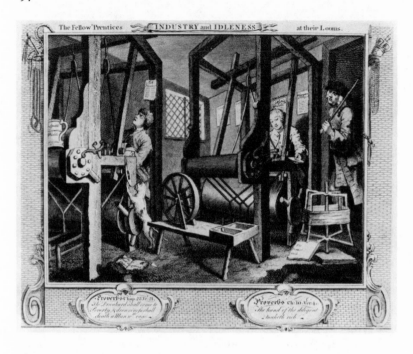

William Hogarth, INDUSTRY AND IDLENESS, *Pl. 1, engr. 1747. The idle apprentice is asleep beneath a ballad version of* MOLL FLANDERS.

work must remain ambiguous, because we accept Moll as a real person and her narrative as the product of her own pen. Since great fiction, by Rader's definition, must announce itself as artifact, *Moll Flanders* is the last of a tradition of "true stories" rather than the forerunner of the novel.[28]

Such a view represents a misunderstanding of Defoe's art as well as of the tradition of literary history which, until the last half of the nineteenth century, always accorded picaresque fiction a secure, if low, position. It also constitutes a misunderstanding of the nature of Defoe's realism. His fictional rhetoric in *Moll Flanders* includes a central character who assumes not merely the particularity of an individual character but also the generality that makes for the prototype of the eternal female. Her endurance in chapbook form, her echo in James Joyce's Molly Bloom and Joyce Cary's Sara Monday of *Herself Surprised* is evidence of this. Moll's language conveys its meanings to the reader through the complexity of word play, innuendo, and ironic asides. And her contradictions, her presentation of various moral views of her actions in a manner that G. S. Starr has properly called "casuistry,"[29] provides a clearer view of the ethical significance of her actions and the ways they are to be judged by the reader than may be found in all but the most didactic novels.

V

I want to conclude this chapter by examining a passage that draws together some of the main ideas I have been discussing. Moll, whose tendency to work alone and whose cautious approach to her "Trade" has enabled her to survive and prosper as the greatest "Artist" of her time, tells how she almost went into a partnership that would have proven disastrous:

I began to think that I must give over the Trade in Earnest; but my Governess, who was not willing to lose me, and expected great Things of me, brought me one Day into Company with a young Woman and a Fellow that went for her Husband, tho' as it appear'd afterwards she was not his Wife, but they were Partners it seems in the Trade they carried on; and Partners in something else too. *In short,* they robb'd together, lay together, were taken together, and at last were hang'd together.

I Came into a kind of League with these two, by the help of my

Governess, and they carried me out into three or four Adventures, where I rather saw them commit some Coarse and unhandy Robberies, in which nothing but a great Stock of impudence on their Side, and gross Negligence on the Peoples Side who were robb'd, could have made them Successful; so I resolv'd from that time forward to be very Cautious how I Adventur'd upon any thing with them; and indeed when two or three unlucky Projects were propos'd by them, I declin'd the offer, and perswaded them against it: One time they particularly propos'd Robbing a Watchmaker of 3 Gold Watches, which they had Ey'd in the Day time, and found the Place where he laid them; one of them had so many Keys of all kinds, that he made no Question to open the Place, where the Watchmaker had laid them; and so we made a kind of an Appointment; but when I came to look narrowly into the Thing, I found they propos'd breaking open the house; and this as a thing out of my Way, I would not Embark in; so they went without me: They did get into the House by main Force, and broke up the lock'd Place where the Watches were, but found but one of the Gold Watches, and a Silver one, which they took, and got out of the House again very clear, but the Family being alarm'd cried out Thieves, and the Man was pursued and taken, the young Woman had got off too, but unhappily was stop'd at a Distance, and the Watches found upon her; and thus I had a second Escape, for they were convicted, and both hang'd, being old Offenders, tho' but young People; as *I said before*, that they robbed together, and lay together, so now they hang'd together, and there ended my new Partnership. [P. 209]

Such a passage would have amused Borrow's old fruit seller. She would have observed the mythic Moll Flanders in the clever thief who is contemptuous of her potential partners' incompetence as well as of the "gross Negligence on the Peoples Side who were robbed." Moll, who usually makes a distinction between herself and those whom she regards as common thieves, demonstrates her superior understanding of her profession and, at least temporarily, emerges superior to the demands of her social environment. She herself seems to be uncertain whether to pity the young couple or to be scornful about their entire way of life. She identifies more with the "Wife," whose capture she views as unfortunate, but on the whole she rises above the situation of her potential "Partnership." That her Governess, still expecting "great Things" of Moll, urged her to join with them suggests that uneasiness in their relationship that gives a certain edge to the genuine affection they feel for each other.

On a somewhat more complex level, the passage moves to a more general type of judgment. With this couple, partnership in crime is also a sexual partnership. Moll's Jemmy never suggests that she join him in such a life. When he has to return to being a highwayman, he parts from Moll affectionately and leaves her behind. But these "Partners" share in everything, including the violent crime of "breaking open the House." It was this kind of crime that brought so much disapprobation on John Sheppard a few years later, for if the locks on a house were to be broken with such ease, who could be safe? The folly of the crime is a reflection of the levity of the couple, and if sad, their punishment is hardly surprising. And given Defoe's continuous metaphor of crime as a form of trade or business, this self-contained little narrative has larger significance as an illustration of all foolish partnerships in mad "Projects."

In speaking of the couple, Moll selects her words carefully, as if she wonders how much she should tell and how to tell it. Just as the "young Woman and a Fellow" do not add up to husband and wife but rather to "Partners," so they are not actually skilled thieves, and the vague partnership in unreal matters ends in their real hanging. Sensing their insubstantiality, Moll is tentative. For all the "help" of her Governess in this arrangement, she only agrees to a "kind of League," and she does not so much join with them in their crimes as allow herself to be "carried" into what she aptly calls "Adventures." The crime that leads to their capture is real in its circumstantial enumeration of the "3 Gold Watches," but the danger is so obvious that Moll merely arranges "a kind of an Appointment." She reports the failure of the scheme with some satisfaction and returns to her clever line on the relationship of the couple in sex, robbery, and hanging. Her final statement on the end of her "Partnership" has to be read as ironic, since she was never truly in anything resembling a relationship of mutual cooperation and trust. And the finality of her last statement has some of the quality of her farewell to the Colchester family with whom she left her children: "and that by the way was all they got by Mrs. Betty" (p. 59). Unfortunately for Moll, she is unable to say good-by to her Governess so effectively.

How many writers can lay claim to greater skill in narrative? Defoe carries his plot forward in time, develops Moll's character in her environment, gives us a vivid sense of the kinds of robberies that were occurring at the time, teaches the reader to worry about housebreaking while warning thieves and businessmen against foolish adventures and especially foolish partnerships. And all of this is accomplished while Defoe is both amusing us and giving us a slight chill of horror at the dismal end of the couple. Critics may talk of Defoe's "unconscious artistry," but of what use such a term may be in speaking of a combination of genius and a lifetime of experience in writing is difficult to comprehend.

5
Crime and Punishment, Event and Myth in *Roxana*

Dor. *Is there no such thing then as an honest Whore?*
M.C. *I have known in my time more Whores than would Hand in Hand made a larger circle than the circumference of* London; *yet never could set sight of the thing called an honest Whore. It is true, young Whores like young Sinners, are oft-times troubled with a weak and distempered Brain, whimsies, reluctancies, sorrow, repentance, and some faint glimpses of what the World calls vertue; but I must tell you, till all these shadows are vanished, they do not deserve the glorious name of Whores.* THE WHORE'S RHETORICK (1683)[1]

ALAN MCKILLOP HAS called *Roxana* "the most neglected of Defoe's major fictions," and although both *Colonel Jack* and *Captain Singleton* are probably even more neglected, *Roxana* has never received the critical attention lavished on *Robinson Crusoe* and *Moll Flanders*. Published in 1724, *Roxana* was the last of his fictional pieces concerned with social life and is usually acknowledged to be both morally and artistically his most complex work. Spiro Peterson has demonstrated Defoe's subtlety in treating the matrimonial theme in relation to the English marriage laws, and John Henry Raleigh has analyzed some elements of Defoe's artistry in *Roxana;* David Higdon and Douglas Brooks have analyzed the novel's structure, and using entirely different methods, George Starr and John Richetti have tried to follow the windings of Roxana's mind.[2] But there has been little agreement on the nature of Defoe's achievement. The character of the heroine, for example, is often confused with that of Moll Flanders, and a recent paperback advertising *Roxana* as "the uninhibited story of literature's most charming, successful and innocent courtesan"[3] is an extreme but by no means uncommon confusion of Defoe's moral intention. But *Roxana* is much more than mediocre pornography, for in this novel Defoe abandoned his emphasis on external reality ("Things")[4] to probe into the mind of a courtesan's progress from the most justifiable sins to the most unnatural, from surrendering her "Virtue" to preserve her life to a partial complicity in the murder of her child. She is neither charming nor innocent, and her success is offset by her final misery. In the following pages I want to discuss *Roxana* as a novel of moral decay and suggest that it represents Defoe's furthest advance in the form of the novel from four vantages: (1) the treatment of narrative point of view; (2) the moral complexity of crime and sin in relation to the interplay of natural, divine, and positive law; (3) the effort to investigate the individual conscience and passions; and (4) the focusing of all the moral and social implications of Roxana's career on a single action—an action existing at once in historical and mythic time.

I

The end of the novel is well known, but since it is necessary to keep Roxana's punishment in mind I shall repeat her last words: "I fell into a dreadful Course of Calamities, and *Amy* also; the very Reverse of our former Good Days; the Blast of Heaven seem'd to follow the Injury done the poor Girl [her daughter], by us both; and I was brought so low again, that my Repentance seem'd to be only the Consequence of my Misery, as my Misery was of my Crime."[5] Although Paul Dottin maintained that this was a somewhat irrelevant tag ending,[6] it is clear that Defoe had Roxana's destruction in mind throughout the novel and that these final words throw doubt on both the sincerity and efficacy of Roxana's repentance. Roxana is not merely an upper-class Moll Flanders; she plunges into moral evils that, by comparison, make Moll's sins appear like the lapses of a saint.

Moll steals and becomes a prostitute because these are her only means of surviving, and she appeals to "necessity" as an excuse for her crimes. So does Roxana, but with this difference: Roxana recognizes her guilt and sins against her "Light." As the preface points out, *"she does not insist upon her Justification. . . . On the contrary, she makes frequent Excursions in a just censuring and condemning her own Practice"* (p. 2). Much of the irony of Moll Flanders depends on the heroine's self-deceptions and self-justifications—her conviction that although she is repentant of her sins, she has merely followed the law of nature that dictates self-preservation. We must look behind Moll's comments and judge them by the standard of natural law that Defoe made one of the moral bases for his novels.[7] But Roxana, who informs the reader that she is "apt to be Satyrical" (p. 6), makes repeated attacks on her own vices as well as on the vices of the men who supported her. Thus, the manner of the narrative reflects the characters of Defoe's two heroines. Whereas Moll, in spite of her self-recriminations, tends to think well of herself and writes with the confidence of her prosperous old age,[8] Roxana tears down all her rationalizations and her narrative reflects something akin to despair. This is important because by announcing that her sins were willful she prevents us from feeling for her the kind of pity that we feel for Moll.

Although it is true that Roxana often tends to involve the reader with her particular way of seeing the world, her ironic remarks on the hypocrisies of society and those who attempt to conceal their immoral acts behind rationalizations which they know to be such, the reader feels uncomfortable—as if he has joined a conspiracy against social conventions without any assurance that he will be given any other set of values to replace them. No wonder Richetti finds her self-control and irony "striking and even frightening."[9]

Defoe was fully aware of the effect to be gained by varying the point of view;[10] he also knew that sin might be presented in a manner that would appeal to our sense of charity for the criminal. Anthony Horneck, the moralist recommended by the ghost of Mrs. Veal, remarked that it was an act of charity to ascribe the sins of others *"either to Education, or to Ignorance, or to the Society, our Neighbour converses with, or to Necessity, or to some other circumstances, which may take off from the greatness of the guilt,"* and that "Whatever is possible in these cases may justly be believed."[11] That Defoe agreed can be seen from his criticism of La Rochefoucauld's theory of self-love not on grounds of error but because it was uncharitable toward human nature: "It is refining too deep upon our Frailties," he remarked, "it is blackening Human Nature, instead of correcting it, and argues a Sourness of Temper, which one would endeavour to conceal from the World, though the Thing should be true."[12] Like La Rochefoucauld, Defoe believed in "the original depravity of human nature" and in man's "propensity to evil rather than to good,"[13] but only in *Roxana* did he explore this "indwelling Sin" to the extent of deliberately alienating the reader's charity for his protagonist.[14]

When Roxana falls into a state of utter destitution through the desertion of her first husband, she finally agrees to save her life by becoming the mistress or, as he insists, "wife" of the Jeweler her landlord. As justification for her action she could rightly plead that she was in the state of necessity, that she was actually the wife of the Jeweler, that she was under an obligation of gratitude. All three of these are valid pleas under the law of nature,[15] yet when her maid, Amy, tries to convince her that she is committing no crime by surrendering her virtue for "Bread" and that the contract which the Jeweler gives her is a genuine marriage agreement, Roxana refuses to accept these arguments.[16] Defoe would have agreed with Amy, but although she violates no law of nature, Roxana insists on her sins: "Well, *Amy, says I,* the Case is as you say, and I think verily I must yield to him; but then, *said I, moved by Conscience,* don't talk any more of your Cant, of its being Lawful that I ought to Marry again . . . ; 'tis all Nonsense . . . for if I yield 'tis in vain to mince the Matter, I am a Whore, *Amy,* neither better nor worse, I assure you" (p. 40). And she argues that this awareness was an additional sin. "I was a double Offender, whatever he was," she explains, "for I was resolv'd to commit the Crime, knowing and owning it to be a Crime; he, if it was true as he said, was fully perswaded it was Lawful" (p. 41). Indeed she repeats this idea of her "double Guilt" (p. 43 et passim) so often that it would seem she wants to leave no doubt in the reader's mind of her complete culpability.[17] Unlike Amy and the Jeweler, Roxana does not feel that the laws of nature can excuse a violation of what she calls "the Laws of God or Man" (p. 38). Defoe would not have criticized Roxana for this scrupulous conscience, but, as we shall see, it is this very sense of guilt that drives Roxana to commit further sins.[18]

Roxana does not try to justify her actions, but she persuades herself that she has yielded from principles of gratitude. Although the Jeweler says that he will not "oppress . . . her Gratitude" (p. 34) by asking favors while she feels an obligation toward him, Roxana has difficulty distinguishing between gratitude and love. And if she does not exculpate herself entirely, she does suggest that hers was a difficult choice. In choosing to plead her case on the virtue that Defoe called "the principal Ingredient, in the Composition of great Souls,"[19] Roxana, nevertheless, takes up an argument that has something of the courtly manner of the *roman galant.*"[20] Saint Evremond's remark that "Women ought not to resist so generous a sentiment as gratitude . . . from a regard for Virtue" embodies exactly the kind of hypocrisy that Defoe attacked in his *Review.*[21] Amy's arguments may be brutal, but Defoe regarded hunger as a far better justification for sin than gratitude.

Even Roxana points out that gratitude is not an excuse, for her conscience must have told her that most of her gratitude ought to have been directed to Heaven: "I shou'd have receiv'd the Mercy thankfully, and apply'd it soberly, to the Praise and Honour of my Maker; whereas by this wicked Course, all the Bounty and Kindness of this Gentleman, became a Snare to me, was a meer Bait to the Devil's Hook; I receiv'd his Kindness at the dear Expence of Body and Soul . . . or, if you will ruin'd my Soul from a Principle of Gratitude, and gave myself up to the Devil, to shew myself grateful to my Benefactor" (p. 38). We must remember that willful sin is an act of ingratitude toward God and that since Roxana accepts the Jeweler's love against the dictates of conscience, she is guilty of this "worst of Crimes."[22]

I have lingered over Roxana's first "crime" because it contrasts with her later sins in being justifiable by natural law and because her "conviction" that she and the Jeweler are merely "Whore and Rogue" leads her to greater sins. The first of these is her deliberate corruption of Amy by tearing off her clothes and throwing her into bed with the Jeweler:

I need say no more, this is enough to convince any body that I did not think him my Husband, and that I had cast off all Principle, and all Modesty, and had effectually stifled Conscience. . . .

Had I look'd upon myself as a Wife, you cannot suppose I would have been willing to have let my Husband lye with my Maid, much less before

Frontispiece to the first edition of THE FORTUNATE MISTRESS [ROXANA] *(1724).*

my Face, for I stood by all the while; but as I thought myself a Whore, I cannot say but that it was something design'd in my Thoughts, that my maid should be a Whore too, and should not reproach me with it. [Pp. 46–47]

Thus for all her middle-class conscience, Roxana becomes the only protagonist in Defoe's fiction who intentionally forces evil on another character. This is a worse crime than any personal sin. As Robert South remarked in a contemporary sermon, "there is as much difference between the pleasure a man takes in his own sins, and that which he takes in other men's, as there is between the wickedness of a man and the wickedness of a devil."[23] Roxana admits that Amy was "less vicious" than she (p. 47), but although moved by her maid's tears and disturbed by the "Aversion" which the Jeweler feels toward Amy afterward, Roxana insists that the polygamous arrangement continue.

II

Defoe's nineteenth-century critics, William Lee, Walter Wilson, and William Minto, tended to group *Roxana* with *Moll Flanders* and *Colonel Jack*. Although obviously disturbed by what they regarded as erotic elements in the novel, they tried to defend it as his most moral work; but they made no distinction between Roxana's first loss of virtue and her later corruption.[24] "Never was a Maid so true to a Mistress" (p. 45), says Roxana of Amy, yet she rewards Amy's fidelity by a singular act of ingratitude. Defoe once wrote that when men act "Ungratefully to those who have serv'd and oblig'd them; so far they deviate into Devils, and will afterwards act like Devils when Opportunity presents."[25] He did not develop his theory of the transformation of human beings into devils until *The Political History of the Devil* (1726), which reveals the influence of Young's *Universal Passion*, but he may have been toying with the idea earlier.[26] Certainly both Roxana and Amy are transformed by their involvement in vice and become increasingly evil. Roxana remarks, "I was not become the Devil's Agent, to make others as wicked as myself" (p. 48), and as Defoe pointed out, human beings can reach depths of evil that can surprise even the devil.[27] Almost all of Defoe's heroes and heroines eventually confront Satan. Moll feels his presence when she thinks of murdering the little girl whom she entices into the alley; Crusoe feels his presence on the island; Captain Singleton dreams of him. In *Roxana*, however, the devil is not Bunyan's demon with wings and cloven hoof, but rather a metaphor for evil, whether he is the "Devil of Poverty" (p. 38) from which Amy's motto "*Comply and live; deny and starve*" (p. 110) rescues her, or the "Jaws of Hell and . . . Power of the real Devil" (p. 38).

When she is about to retire from her life as a courtesan, Roxana tells the reader that she was motivated by the three vices of avarice, vanity, and pride:[28]

> as Necessity first debauch'd me and Poverty made me a Whore at the Beginning; so excess of Avarice for getting Money, and excess of Vanity, continued me in the Crime, not being able to resist the Flatteries of Great Persons; being call'd the finest Woman in *France*, being caress'd by a Prince; and afterwards, I had Pride enough to expect, and Folly enough to believe, tho' indeed without ground, by a Great Monarch? These were my Baits, these the Chains by which the Devil held me bound. [P. 202]

Of her avarice little need be said. There are suggestions of its origins in her love for the Jeweler, and both her pride and avarice are satisfied by her next love, the Prince. She reveals her greatest affection for him when he gives her a diamond necklace, telling the reader how she is "all on fire with the Sight" (p. 73). This mingling of love and avarice is also present in Moll's first love, but without those elements of affected sensibility that occasionally appear in *Roxana*.[29] Moll never has lines like Roxana's remark, "I satisfy'd myself . . . that, as it was all irresistable, so it was all lawful; for that Heaven would not suffer us to be punish'd for that which it was not possible for us to avoid." Roxana herself cannot help referring to these thoughts as "Absurdities." Her conscience remains unappeased, and she considers going to a priest to rid herself of guilt by Catholic casuistry (pp. 68–69).[30]

But the affair with the Prince chiefly stirs her vanity, and she even tries to justify some of her actions on the grounds that "tho' Poverty and Want is an irresistible Temptation to the Poor, Vanity and Great Things are as irresistible to others" (p. 64). That Roxana is merely trying to rationalize her vices can be seen from her treatment of the kindly Dutchman who rescues her from destruction. She repays him first by cheating him of the money he has lost on her account and finally, after many years, by marrying him under the guise of an honest woman. "It is most certain, that speaking of Originals, I was the Source and Spring of all that Trouble and Vexation to this honest Gentleman," Roxana confesses, "and as it was afterwards in my Power to have made him full Satisfaction, and did not, I cannot say but I added Ingratitude to all the rest of my Follies" (p. 135). After committing this "worse of Crimes" (pp. 170–71) once more and engaging in an unnatural defense of sexual freedom for women, she leaves him to find her "Element" in the vicious court of Charles II.[31] Here she dances lasciviously, allows her apartments to be used for gambling and "what they call'd a Party" (p. 172), becomes mistress to the King, and finally abandons her life as a public courtesan only after she is wealthy enough to retire and give up her Lord, whose sexual perversions have disgusted her.

Although retired from public life, Roxana at fifty is a victim of her vitiated passions. Her "Lunatick" pride impels her to become a member of the very nobility she has preyed on, and she searches after the Prince as a likely person to marry and ennoble her. Fortunately for him he has escaped by his repentance, and we can perceive some of Roxana's depravity in Amy's attempts to console her mistress for the loss of the Prince: *"Law'd Madam!* never be concern'd at it; you see he is gotten among the Priests and I suppose, they have saucily impos'd some Pennance upon him; and, *it may-be,* sent him of [sic] an Errand barefoot, to some *Madonna* or *Nosterdame* or other; and he is off of his Amours for the present; I'll warrant you, he'll be as wicked again as ever he was, when he is got thorow-well, and gets but out of their Hands again: I hate this out-o'-Season Repentance" (pp. 237–38). Pride and ambition have brought Roxana close to insanity, and she seeks solace in marrying the Dutch Merchant.[32] By purchasing titles of nobility, her new husband makes her a Baronet's Lady in England and a Countess in Holland. There she lives in outward prosperity for two years, but she is afflicted by an inner misery, a "Dart struck into the Liver" and a "secret Hell within" (p. 260), which spoils her happiness and leaves her in a "constant Terror" that she will be destroyed by the wrath of Heaven.

That Roxana's misery arises from one of her few good actions is not without irony. Careless of her illegitimate children, Roxana displays a genuine interest, affection, and generosity toward the children of her first marriage. She abandons them only under the shadow of starvation, and on returning to England rescues them from poverty and provides the money to educate them. Eventually she establishes her son as a merchant, but one of her daughters, Susan, insists on discovering who their benefactor is. She believes that her mother is alive and wants to find her even at the cost of her own and her mother's destruction.

Susan is not to be regarded as an innocent, loving daughter seeking maternal affection, for Roxana has failed her both as a parent and as a member of the upper classes. Defoe insisted that it was the parent's duty to provide an example for her children, but Susan has worked as a maid in Roxana's establishment in Pall Mall and is fully aware of the kind of life her mother has lived.[33] As early as 1698, in his pamphlet *The Poor Man's Plea . . . for a Reformation of Manners*, Defoe complained that the vices of the rich were responsible for corrupting the manners of the poor.[34] Ironically enough, Roxana has corrupted her daughter by her example in much the same way she corrupted Amy. At the end all three are possessed by violent emotions: Roxana, loving her daughter but wishing her dead; Amy, loving Roxana and ready to murder Susan to save her mistress even at the expense of gaining her hatred; and Susan, searching for her mother partly from affection and partly from a desire to get something—perhaps money or power.

With "a kind of a Smile, or a Grin" (p. 270) Susan suggests to Amy that Roxana is her mother, which assures Roxana that the "sharp Jade" knows "that her Mother had play'd the Whore" (p. 269). But when Amy concludes that it will be "absolutely necessary to murther her," a violent scene occurs between Roxana and her companion of twenty-five years in which the language suggests their transformation into devils:

That Expression fill'd me with Horror; all my Blood ran chill in my Veins, and a Fit of trembling seiz'd me, that I cou'd not speak a good-while; at last, What is the Devil in you, *Amy, said I?* Nay, nay, *says she,* let it be the Devil, or not the Devil, if I thought she knew one tittle of your History, I wou'd dispatch her if she were my own Daughter a thousand times; and I, *says I in a Rage,* as well as I love you, wou'd be the first that shou'd put the Halter about your Neck and see you hang'd, with more Satisfaction than ever I saw you in my Life; nay, *says I,* you wou'd not live to be hang'd, I *believe*, I shou'd cut your Throat with my own Hand; . . . with that, I call'd her cursed Devil, and bade her get out of the Room. [P. 271]

But Roxana is now married to an upstanding middle-class merchant to whom she has surrendered control of her wealth, and she must maintain her reputation by concealing her past. "I think the D——l is in that young Wench" (p. 272), says Amy, lamenting their future ruin. In their eyes, at least, Susan is a scourge from hell.[35]

Roxana is also punished in another way, for while fearing to become the "Girl's Vassal" (p. 280), she is moved by a strong natural affection for Susan. When the "Devil" lays a snare for her and she meets Susan on the ship that was to carry her to the safety of Holland, Roxana feels an almost overwhelming urge to embrace her:

No pen can describe, no Words can express, *I say*, the strange Impression which this thing made upon my Spirits; I felt something shoot thro' my Blood; my Heart flutter'd; my Head flash'd, and was dizzy, and all within me, *as I thought*, turn'd about, and much ado I had, not to abandon myself to an Excess of Passion at the first Sight of her, much more when my Lips touch'd her Face; I thought I must have taken her in my Arms, and kiss'd her again a thousand times, whether I wou'd or no. [P. 277]

The impending murder of Susan and Roxana's ability to control an external display of her emotions prevent the scene from slipping into either sentimentality or melodrama. Roxana tells us how she "rous'd up . . . her Judgment, and shook it off" (p. 277), and she informs the reader that she "shou'd have shed but very few Tears" for Susan "had she dropp'd into the Grave by any fair Way" (p. 302). In spite of her affection, Roxana regards her daughter as an "Evil-Spirit" haunting her life and does nothing very definite to prevent Amy from carrying through her murderous plans.

III

The final section of the novel reflects Defoe's growing interest in psychology. In 1723, the year before he wrote *Roxana*, in a work assigned to him by Professor Moore, Defoe speculated on the

"Impossibility to us of knowing the Secrets of one anothers Hearts." "Words," he continued, ". . . do not necessarily convey the true Sentiment of Man's Mind; which is therefore, to every Man upon Earth but himself, absolutely Undiscoverable and certainly known to God alone."[36] And in one of his journals he pointed out the advantages of this: "How happy . . . is it for the greatest Part of Mankind, that Nature has made no Glass Beehives to the Heart; that it is not in Man to know what is in Man! What a Sink of Wickedness! What a Hell of Treachery and Falshood would be every Day the subject of our Speculations! . . . Blessed Fate of Men! How happy are we, that we see no more than the Outsides of one another! And where is the Man who could bear an Inspection into the Inside of his Soul?"[37] These thoughts may have been in Defoe's mind when he was writing *Roxana*, for the novel represents his most determined effort to look into the heart of a character.

The result is the unpleasant personality of Roxana, whose soul is indeed a "Sink of Wickedness" and who lacks Moll Flanders's warmth and humor. Her pervasive ironic tone is turned against herself and her motives as well as against her society and proceeds from a form of self-hatred. With the exception of forcing Amy into bed with the Jeweler, Roxana is passively evil. Whereas Moll and Jack wander through the streets of London and Singleton scours the oceans in search of something to steal, Roxana merely waits for the Jeweler, Prince, Merchant, King, and Lord to visit her with their gifts. Jonathan Bishop has argued that for Defoe and all his heroes and heroines "the adventure is the archetype of all human activity; the going forth of the mind against a hostile nature."[38] But Roxana defies any attempt to classify her as an adventurous heroine, and if Defoe sometimes appears to regard activity as a cardinal virtue (it is almost the only virtue displayed by Captain Singleton), Roxana's passivity has the effect of emphasizing her immorality.

Roxana also lacks that "Courage of Constitution" which distinguishes all of Defoe's lower-class characters, and is the most extreme example of the anxiety which Benjamin Boyce identified as the dominant emotion in all of Defoe's heroes and heroines.[39] If we compare her to Amy, we can see the difference at once. Amy actively advocates Roxana's surrender to the Jeweler, acts as

Roxana's agent in all her affairs, and finally decides that the only way to aid her mistress is by murdering Susan. When their ship is caught in a violent storm on the voyage to Holland, Roxana remarks on the difference between them:

> I know not what ail'd me, not I; but *Amy* was much more penitent at Sea, and much more sensible of her Deliverance when she Landed, was safe, than I was; I was in a kind of Stupidity, I know not well what to call it; I had a Mind full of Horrour in the time of the Storm, and saw Death before me, as plainly as *Amy*, but my Thoughts got no Vent as *Amy*'s did; I had a silent sullen kind of Grief, which cou'd not break out either in Words or Tears, and which was, therefore, much the worse to bear. [Pp. 128–29]

Amy, like Robinson Crusoe, is able to relieve her anxiety by action, whereas Roxana, whatever her inner feelings, preserves an outward control.

At first sight this quality may seem admirable. Like so many writers of the eighteenth century, Defoe praised the man who could keep "his rising Passions at a full Command,[40] but Roxana's control is different from that stoic prudence and "*Coldness of the Passions*" which, following Pufendorf, he urged his readers to emulate.[41] Ernest Baker and Willa Cather objected to Roxana's "antiseptic" qualities as a failure of Defoe's art because *they* failed to see the kind of character Defoe was attempting to create. She does not possess a philosophic calm, but rather that "Stupidity" and "sullen silent kind of Grief" which Defoe associated with damnation and despair.[42] Of the qualities that Defoe thought "heroic,"[43] Roxana merely possesses some "capacity" and "application," but these qualities, as Defoe reminded his readers, were also those that the devil might claim as well.[44] It is no accident that, despite her forceful intelligence, this "Queen of Whores" (p. 82) is Defoe's least attractive protagonist.

Her final disaster is left in doubt, but among the many hints that Defoe threw out in the course of the novel, the most provocative concerns a betrayal by her own conscience. In *Captain Singleton*, Defoe showed his hero waking from terrifying dreams and talking in his sleep about his crimes; similarly in the year before the publication of *Roxana*, he devoted an issue of *Applebee's Journal* to the power of conscience and the story of a man who confessed to a murder by a slip of the tongue.[45] Several years later he expanded this theme in an entire section of his *Essay on the History and Reality of Apparitions,* describing how the soul of the murderer becomes a "mere Mass of Horror and Confusion" gnawed at by "*a Worm that never dies*" until he either commits suicide or relieves his conscience by confessing. Heaven withdraws its protection and the criminal is "haunted with the Ghosts of his own Imagination." The attending spirits open "the Sluices of the Soul" and abandon him to "an enraged Conscience . . . a Flood of unsufferable Grief, . . . Rage, Anguish, Self-reproach, too late Repentance, and final Desperation."[46]

Dostoevski has made the process familiar to modern readers through the characters of both Raskolnikov and Svidrigaylov. Like them, Roxana has terrible dreams of her murdered daughter and feels an urge to confess. She regrets once more that she "was not a *Roman-Catholic*" even if her confessor had given her some terrible penance. "However, as I had none of the recourse," she laments, "so I had none of the Absolution by which the Criminal confessing, goes away comforted; but I went about with a Heart loaded with Crime, and altogether in the dark, as to what I was to do; and in this Condition I languish'd near two Years; I may well call it languishing, for if Providence had not reliev'd me, I shou'd have died in little time" (p. 265).

Defoe's Christian charity was exemplary when he insisted that "Heaven itself receives those who sincerely repent into the same state of acceptance as if they had not sinned at all." But he also insisted that the "main design" of a person's life be "up right."[47] Some, like Jonathan Wild and Captain Gow, "sin a Knot too much," and it is significant that although Roxana speaks of Providence relieving her, she is not shown undergoing a repentance that includes both a love of God and detestation of her crimes.[48] We cannot be absolutely certain that Roxana is in a state of despair, but certainly her narrative lacks both joy and hope.

IV

I have tried to offer evidence that the plot of *Roxana* revolves about the decline of Roxana's moral character, a decline that is contrasted with her worldly success. But although the focus of the novel is mainly on Roxana's hardening conscience, the course of her career implies the moral decline of the entire society. The central scenes of the novel, Roxana's two performances before the court in her Turkish costume, result in her achieving the heights of her ambition by becoming mistress of the King. Her dance, her Turkish costume, and her christening bring together the two satirical elements of the novel: the attack on the sexual immorality of the Restoration and with it the implied comparison with contemporary morality; and the attack on disguise and deception. By this device Defoe uses the theme of moral corruption to unify *Roxana* in much the same way that the theme of isolation unifies *Robinson Crusoe*.

Defoe's foreshadowing of this scene is subtler than most of the mechanical predictions of relating events "hereafter" or in their "Place" which appear throughout the novel. At the beginning of her narrative, Roxana predicts that her dancing will play an important part in her life. "Being *French* Born," she remarks, "I danced, *as some say*, naturally, lov'd it extremely, and sung well also, and so well, that, *as you will hear*, it was afterwards some Advantage to me" (p. 6). She is attracted to her first husband mainly because he "danc'd well", her crime against Amy occurs after a night of dancing, and she learns her Turkish dance and songs when she is mistress of the Prince in Italy discovering the "loose Life" of the women of Naples. Her promise to tell the reader how she used her knowledge of Turkish dancing to her "Advantage on an extraordinary Occasion, some Years after" (p. 102) occurs in the middle of her praise of Italian luxury.[49]

When Roxana dances at her party and a courtier "cry'd out, *Roxana! Roxana!* by ———, with an Oath" (p. 176), the narrator gains an identity that had been lacking in the novel up to this point. Ian Watt has suggested how important the names of characters are in early fiction, and Defoe never used a name with richer implications than Roxana.[50] It has usually been suggested that the source of the name is the *Memoirs of Count Grammont*, which refers to the actress Hester Davenport who, according to Boyer's translation, acted the role of Roxana in Nathaniel Lee's *Rival Queens* and became the mistress of the Earl of Oxford.[51] But the courtier who "Christen'd" her is supposed to be thinking in terms of Turkey rather than of a stage play.

One of the major sources of Defoe's scene, an adventure in Richard Head and Francis Kirkman's *The English Rogue,* throws some light on the significance of this moment in the novel. Mary, a prostitute who takes genuine pleasure in her profession, tells her companions of an affair she once had with a lover of a literary turn. He woos her with lines from Ovid, finds a connection between his own affair and parts of Beaumont and Fletcher's *Philaster,* and is so entranced by Hester Davenport's Roxolana in Sir William Davenant's *The Siege of Rhodes* that he willingly pays £20 to Mary when she offers to bring "Roxolana in his arms." Mary has a tailor, who supplies costumes to the theaters, copy the proper costume, and after applying the proper cosmetics, she appears before him as Roxolana. After discovering that the Turkish princess is actually Mary in disguise, he confesses, *"I am very well satisfied therein, and am now more glad that you have found out this way to please me, than if I enjoyed the very party her self,"* a statement which is hardly surprising from someone who prefers art to life.[52] The dancing, eating, and sex that follow are significant for Defoe's novel:

Our Collation being ended, I and my attendants danced, and spent much time in such kind of divertisements; but I saw that my friend was impatient till bed time came, that he might have me, his beloved *Princess,* in his arms: we were waited on with all manner of state, and had Musick attending us, not only all the time we were up, but also when we were in bed: they being placed in the Chamber adjoyning to our lodgings, where they played for two hours space after we were retired.

The strength of imagination was much, for as my bedfellow imagined that he had a *Princess* in his arms so I conceited my self to be little less: great was the pleasure, I received from, and gave to my bedfellow, for we were both in the flower of our age, he being about twenty, and I eighteen, we had both equal desires, and thought of nothing but pleasure.[53]

I do not feel that Defoe was trying to evoke a literary allusion as a point of reference for his audience. The real value of this source is that it tells us much about Defoe's creative imagination. Although the character of Roxolana is Turkish, Mary's performance represents a disguise of a disguise. The hearty libertinism of her narrative is turned inside out in Defoe's version. And finally, it shows that Defoe's major source was written in and about the Restoration and that the realistic surface recreates the manners and morals of the time of Charles II.

But just as Defoe was trying to evoke a period that could function both as history and as an image of contemporary life, so he also aimed at creating, in the figure of Roxana, a quintessential courtesan rather than any single historical mistress.[54] Hester Davenport was famous for being, perhaps, the first actress of some note on the English stage and for becoming mistress of Aubrey de Vere, Earl of Oxford. She provides Roxana with a name and a possible future, but for Roxana's character, Defoe drew on a melange of the King's mistresses. Like Mademoiselle Bardou she is known for her dance, and like Nell Gwynn she refers to herself as a "Protestant Whore" (p. 69), a comment few readers could have missed. She resembles the Duchess of Portsmouth not only in her French origins but also in going through a mock marriage ceremony before becoming a mistress.[55] Most of all, she resembles Charles's last mistress of note, the Duchess of Mazarin, who mingled Italian and French manners, who insisted on her freedom to choose lovers, and who was satirized in a poem attributed to Rochester as the most flagrant of Charles's concubines.[56] But, as I have stated, an attempt to identify Roxana with any single person would be an error and would miss Defoe's point. He was trying to show a court and a society in which conventional marital relationships had been replaced by various forms of polygamy and polyandry. And we must remember that Roxana feels that this is her "Element" (p. 181). Although Roxana may be thinking of Hester Davenport when she worries about becoming "a mere Roxana" (p. 182), Defoe was also drawing on a rich literary background for his name. In Richard Knolles's *Lives and Conquests of the Othoman Kings and Emperors*, Roxolana, the wife of Solyman, was depicted as ambitious, "subtill," and, most of all, deceitful. Under her portrait in the edition of 1638 was the inscription:

> To fairest looks trust not too farre, nor yet to beauty brave
> For hateful thoughts so finely maskt, their deadly poyson have.[57]

Both William Davenant's *Siege of Rhodes* and Roger Boyle's *Mustapha*, plays in which Hester Davenport performed, drew on Knolles for their depiction of Roxolana, and certainly Defoe's

Roxana associates the name with a type of stage heroine.[58] She pretends to be indignant that her daughter might think that she was "some *French* Comedian, *that is to say,* a Stage *Amazon,* that put on a counterfeit Dress to please the Company, such as they us'd in the Play of *Tamerlane* at *Paris,* or some such" (p. 289). Roxana's vagueness is deliberate. There is no Roxana in *Tamerlane,* but the name Roxana or Roxolana suggested a type of woman not so different from Defoe's heroine, who engages in a defense of sexual liberty, speaks in "Amazonian Language" about her finances, and accepts the murder of her daughter as a means of ensuring her safety. Many of these elements appear in the Roxolana of Knolles as well as in the Roxana of Lee's *Rival Queens,* in Racine's *Bajazet,* and even in Montesquieu's *Persian Letters,* where the slave girl Roxana revolts against the restraints of the harem in the name of liberty.[59]

Roxana then might well appear as a Turkish lady in a contemporary romance, but we must not forget that Roxana is actually French and that her dance is also French. Like the pseudo-Persian costumes of the court of Charles, her dance is an unnatural parody of the dances of the Armenian and Georgian maidens who perform before her. "They danc'd three times all-alone, for nobody indeed cou'd dance with them," she admits. "The Novelty pleas'd truly, but yet there was something wild and *Bizarre* in it, because they really acted to the Life the barbarous Country whence they came; but as mine had the *French* Behaviour under the *Mahometan* Dress, it was every way as new, and pleas'd much better, indeed" (p. 179). This is not so much a theory of aesthetics as a moral commentary, for Defoe frequently drew on primitivistic ideas in attacking the vices of society. The Turks and savage nations, he argued, follow the laws of nature and "act more like Men of Reason than we do."[60]

In creating his mythic courtesan, his "Queen of Whores," out of so many elements, Defoe seemed reluctant to place her in any definite time between his own period and that of the Restoration. As a result, he resorted to a curious combination of mythic synchronic time and the particular serial chronology of history.[61] He might have followed the historical pattern of *Memoirs of a Cavalier* or that of *A Journal of the Plague Year* with its dynamic interaction between past and present, but instead of staying with the historical moment, he decided, in defiance of all artistic probability, to stretch out time in all directions. Perhaps he was simply trying to protect himself from charges of libel,[62] of maybe he no longer found a reference to past history sufficiently vivid. But whatever his reason, the dates that emerge from the novel defy any notion of history the reader might have, while the actual experience of reading Roxana's account provides a realistic sense of growth, movement, and change. In some sense, the Restoration functions as a historical allegory for the reign of George I, but while Roxana's career as a courtesan resonates with moral significance, Defoe leaves the historical parallels to the informed contemporary reader.

Roxana's costume is symbolic of the masquerading of Charles's court and, by implication, the court of George I. Defoe may have been thinking of Rochester's disguises when he wrote several years later in an attack on his age:

Thus we live in a general disguise, and like the masquerades, every man dresses himself up in a particular habit, not two appear alike in the whole place; and that the simile may be perfect, the humour carries it on to the minutest part; as the habits are not alike, so they are always particularly remarkable for being directly opposite to the person they cover; the phlegmatic dresses *a la sanguine,* the sober mimic the drunkard, the chaste chooses to dress *a la courtisane,* the atheist puts on the *religieuse,* the Christian has the vest and the turban, and the Quaker a habit from the theatre.[63]

Defoe attacked contemporary masquerade as leading inevitably to the decline of sexual morality, and he once sketched the progress of a harlot, beginning with a masquerade and ending with her death, "a Prey to most corroding Diseases."[64] Like Pufendorf, Bayle, and Mandeville, Defoe believed that modesty was merely custom while shame was a passion.[65] To mask and disguise was to hide the visible sign of shame which innocent girls feel, but the newly christened Roxana who finds that she is in her "Element" in the court of Charles has no innocence to lose. Her disguise summarizes all that is evil in herself and in the court.

As might be predicted from Defoe's attack on the "general disguise" of the age, Roxana assumes her opposite identity when she retires from her life as a public courtesan. She assumes the

dress of the Quakers and adds hypocrisy to her sins by pretending to an outward sign of modesty and religion. But she preserves
her Turkish costume and cannot resist the folly of showing it to
the Quakeress and her husband with the admission that it would
not be considered "a decent Dress in this Country." The dress
has a curious effect, for the Quakeress is impressed and remarks
that "if such a Dress shou'd come to be worn here, . . . she
shou'd be tempted not to dress in the Quakers' Way any-more"
(p. 247). Roxana's fondness for this costume is indicative of her
regret for the loss of "all the Gayety and Glory" of court life (p.
237).

She promises that the reader "will hear more of" this dress (p.
248), and it becomes the most important clue in Susan's identification of Roxana as her mother. In one of the best scenes in the
novel Susan tells proudly of how Roxana danced in her costume
to the applause of the masked courtiers. The Quakeress is
shocked by the thought that the King "wou'd disguise himself"
(p. 288), but Susan is fascinated by this event. The story of Roxana's dance is told because Susan's friend believes that it would
amuse Roxana. "That's a damn'd Lye" (p. 286), Roxana thinks to
herself. Yet as the narrative continues, she proudly relives the
moment: "I cannot help confessing what a Reserve of Pride still
was left in me; and tho' I dreaded the Sequel of the Story, yet
when she talk'd how handsome and how fine a Lady this *Roxana*
was, I cou'd not help being pleas'd and tickl'd with it; and put in
Questions two or three times of how handsome she was? and was
she really so fine a Woman as they talk'd of? *and the like,* on
purpose to hear her repeat what the People's Opinion of me was,
and how I had behav'd" (p. 287). The reader is reminded of
Roxana's dance then, both in her performing for the merchant
and in Susan's narrative; it becomes the focal point of Roxana's
own immorality as well as that of society. Although Susan's admiration for Roxana may seem innocent enough, it includes an
admiration of her mother's vicious life. The Quaker tries to convince Susan that Roxana is not her mother on the grounds that
"the Lady at her house was a Person above any Disguises" (pp.
306–7). But disguise and deception are the essence of Roxana's
life—a life that she cannot abandon entirely, precisely because it
was so flattering to her pride and vanity. These are the sins that

lead to the discovery of the Turkish dress, and this, in turn, leads to the murder of Susan.[66]

Bonamy Dobrée has maintained that, with the possible exception of *Roxana*, Defoe's novels lack any true form: "there is no structure in the sense of change of speed, no tension, no preparation for a scene followed by that scene; no climax, and therefore no emotional node."[67] Defoe tried to remedy this lack in *Roxana*, and at times he shows surprising skill and artistry. He also avoided the temptation to moralize directly on the luxury and vice of the court; he didn't have to moralize, for his heroine embodied his vision of a corrupt society.

What prevents *Roxana* from being Defoe's masterpiece is the truncated ending. Robert Hume has argued that the novel has succeeded in making its statement and that "neither flat narration nor melodrama could equal the sheer terse scariness of the last two paragraphs as they stand,"[68] but we never learn how Roxana is eventually brought to final misery, how the external greatness of her life as a Countess comes to match her internal sufferings. The reason that Defoe decided not to continue has produced various speculations. Dottin argued that Defoe had grown tired of his story, McKillop and Dobrée that he was faced with moral and technical problems that exceeded his grasp, and Boyce that Defoe was so personally involved in Roxana's anxieties and future disaster that he could not continue.[69] It seems doubtful that Defoe would become bored by the most gripping psychological situation he ever created, but certainly he may have felt that to continue the story of Roxana would involve him in a project he found difficult both as an artist and as a man. He was probably influenced by two other considerations: he had exhausted the serious sociological message which he felt to be the justification for fiction;[70] and he thought that the tracing of Roxana's decline into despair and misery was not the kind of material his audience found of interest in a novel. In his *Family Instructor,* Defoe traced the career of a disobedient son through the horrors of sickness, the amputation of his arm, and his death "in a miserable condition, atheistical and impenitent"; but fiction was different from books of moral conduct. "As there is no instructing you, without pleasing you," he wrote to his audience, "and no pleasing you but in your own way, we must go on in that way;

the understanding must be refined by allegory and enigma; . . . in a word, the manners must be reformed in masquerade, devotion quickened by the stage, not the pulpit, and wit be brightened by satires upon sense."[71]

Despite the abrupt ending, *Roxana* reveals more careful workmanship, if not greater genius, than Defoe displayed in any other novel. The interplay between the individual conscience and the laws of God, nature, and men creates a psychological and moral complexity that is unique in early fiction; and these elements are brilliantly unified by Roxana's dance and christening. Even in its unfinished state *Roxana* may be said to approach that "seriousness of art" that critics have found wanting in his other novels.[72]

6

"Appearances of Truth": Defoe, the Literature of Crime, and the Novel

Nay, so little Ground has there been for them, that except that there was such a Man as Jonathan Wild, *that he was born at* Wolverhampton, *liv'd in the* Old-Bayley, *was call'd a Thief Catcher, and was Hang'd at* Tyburn, *there is not one Story printed of him that can be call'd Truth, or that is not mingled up with so much Falshood and Fable as to smother and drown that little Truth which is at the bottom of it.* DEFOE, *The True and Genuine Account of the Life and Actions of the Late Jonathan Wild*[1]

AMONG THE MANY forms of narrative that existed during the Restoration, few were more popular than the various accounts of crime, and few have been more neglected. I don't mean that there have not been studies of criminal accounts as sources for fiction[2] but that such accounts seem not to have been examined as a self-contained system of narrative with its own genres—reports on the crimes committed, accounts of the capture of the criminals, trials, descriptions of prisons, speeches from the cell or at the gallows, reports from attending clergymen on the psychological and spiritual state of the criminal at his or her death, and finally, a criminal biography of some length incorporating a summary of the entire career of the malefactor.

The reason for this omission during the eighteenth century is obvious: whereas there existed a considerable body of critical opinion on the art of writing history and biography and even a growing awareness of the necessity to shape travel literature, the complex of genres cited above constituted a system that was sometimes thought antithetical to the aims of art. Swift's Hack in *A Tale of a Tub* could see the pattern clearly enough to place it alongside fanatical religion and the slapdash theater of strolling players as a potential area for bad art and self-expression of an equally disastrous kind. Fielding adopted Swift's view in utilizing the career of Jonathan Wild as an occasion for literary parody and for a commentary on English society and politics. For both Swift and Fielding, the artistic potential in such material represented the wrong kind of art—an art of realistic re-creation in which some of the pathos of real life might dominate the shaping powers of the writer, leaving the moral statement uncontrolled and the experience of the reader necessarily ambiguous. When Charles Lamb praised Defoe's fiction as "Appearances of Truth," producing a reading experience similar to "reading evidence in a court of justice," he was expressing an admiration that was not out of line with romantic criticism.[3] But in artistic circles of the previous century, such aesthetic judgment belonged only to that small number of critics who could see some good qualities in Dutch landscapes and in the work of Rembrandt.[4] As might be expected of an age that produced a Chardin, a Hogarth, and a Greuze and specialized in realistic portraiture and *trompe l'oeil* effects, some such admirers did exist, but their influence on contemporary critical theory was slow to emerge.

Yet Lamb's comparison is richly suggestive for both fiction and genuine accounts of crime. It was Edmund Burke who remarked that the impact of witnessing a genuine hanging was such as to make the tragedies of the theater seem tame.[5] And if Burke could find some similarity between the audiences at these two spectacles, it is not too much to believe that the reading audience for the lives of criminals was similar to that which read fiction. Certainly there was a considerable degree of shaping in the historical accounts to make them competitive with fiction. The editor-author of *A Collection of State-Trials and Proceedings upon High Treason and Other Crimes*, which appeared originally in 1719, published an abridged edition in the following year, *Tryals for High Treason and Other Crimes*, with an introduction in which he argued that accounts of trials might be improved by cutting and shaping the "infinite Variety of Tragick Scenes. Not fictions, form'd only to amuse and please, of which our English Gentry seem so fond, but such as are supported by uncontested Truth."[6] It was the "Truth" in the trials that would add to the general pleasure of reading a detailed narrative and make them more "entertaining" than works like *Robinson Crusoe*, England's first sustained work of realistic fiction that had appeared, significantly enough, in the same year as the folio edition of the State Trials. I will have more to say about these trials and the introduction to the abridgment later, but one should note its editor's careful statement that his work is not intended for specialists in the legal system but for the general reader.

I

And here it is very Remarkable, That tho' during this Intercourse of Mr. Wild among these loose People . . . many of them dayly fell into the Hand of Justice, and some went off the Stage, the High Road, (as they call it) that is to say, by the Gallows; yet none of them had any thing to say to Jonathan, or to his She Friend, Mrs. Milliner: but these always did their Business so Clean, with such Subtilty, and so much to the Advantage of the Criminals, that it was of no Use to them to charge him or her with any Thing. DEFOE, *The True and Genuine Account of the Life and Actions of the Late Jonathan Wild, p. 6.*

Discovering the proper tone, selecting the right trials, fashioning narrative and character was part of the art of such accounts as it was to be that of writing literary fictions, and the two modes developed side by side, not without occasional confusion and mingling. Defoe's role in this confusion was vital. His specialty was fiction, but as the master journalist of the early eighteenth century, he usually saw and exploited the fictive potential in real events only after he had written about them in brief notices or in the form of letter-essays in *Mist's* or *Applebee's* weekly papers. He did not invent the trial or criminal biography as modes, but he did help to give the complex of genres surrounding criminal accounts a particular shape. His fictions appeared concurrently with the sudden surge in crimes of all sorts during the period spanning 1715 to 1725, and there is much to be said for Defoe as the mythologist of this crime wave. But criminal accounts were common enough in the Restoration and before.

What is unquestionably true, however, is that such accounts

gradually became more sophisticated in handling narrative. They even became part of theatrical comedy when, in 1697, Mary Pix used the hawking of a typical production, *A Full and True Relation of a Horrid and Bloody Murther, Committed on the Body of Mrs. Arabella Venturewell, a Young Lady, by One 'Squire Cheatall, and His Man Gentil,* as a device for frightening one of her comic villains.[7] The work itself tells how the two supposed murderers locked Arabella in a dark closet, cut her to pieces, and tried to get rid of the remains at Chelsea-Reach. Such works, sold just as this one, by a boy walking along the streets, had a remarkable popularity. Though filled with the kind of circumstantial realism typical of the form, *A Full and True Relation* was, of course, a work of fiction. Even in a decade specializing in realistic comedy, an audience accustomed to such productions must have considered it a nice comic touch.

In addition to such broadsides and chapbooks, which go back to the earlier days of the century, works like John Reynolds's tremendous *Triumphs of God's Revenge against the Crying and Execrable Sin of Murther,* with their mixture of narrative and moralizing, continued to be printed through the eighteenth century and into the next. But some changes occurred during the Restoration. In 1679 *God's Revenge against the Abominable Sin of Adultery* was attached to Reynolds's work with illustrations that were explicit enough to appeal more to the casual pornographer than to the moralist. The stories do moralize on the sexual escapades of the characters, but the line between these accounts and the similarly illustrated *Trials for Adultery; or, The History of Divorces,* accounts taken from cases in the ecclesiastical courts or Doctors Commons and published in six volumes in 1779, is not as great as might be expected. And in the final section of *God's Revenge against . . . Adultery,* a "Dutch History," the line between exemplary sermon and picaresque fiction is almost nonexistent. From moralized tales of murder and high tales of adultery, the reader is led into the realistically narrated tale of a miner's daughter (with some suggestions of higher origins) taken into the family of a "Lady," renamed Judirina, and led through a series of adventures that foreshadow many of the elements of *Moll Flanders* and *Roxana.* At one point Judirina even assumes the disguise of a "Daughter of a Gentleman in Flanders," and in another of her adventures she calls herself Rosana. Her end is more like that of Laclos's Madame Merteuil than that of either of Defoe's heroines, and the description is vividly realistic in the manner of the picaresque or of contemporary antifeminist satire:

This may let us see of what filthy matter the greatest beauty of flesh is made: Rosana's fair and plump cheeks were now grown lean and hagged, the smouth skin shrivelled, and discoloured, those bright and twinkling stars, that had so many charms, and so much lustre, were now sunk, and wholly obscured, grown limped, and running with matter: her Teeth which were like orient pearl for whiteness, were black, and fallen out, her pretty mouth disfigur'd, her nose eaten quite away, and a running sore left only in the place of it: her angellick voyce, now odious and disagreeing, the pallat of her mouth, and Epiglottis being eaten away, with a Cancer: her whole body covered with boyles, botches, and blayns, that she was a most deplorable, and loathed spectacle, shunned of others, and hated by her self.[8]

Not only is the realism startling here and in other sections, but there is a new kind of fictional metaphysic at work. Instead of the continual reminder of God's presence and impending revenge, the author speculates on cause and effect as if the world were not entirely under God's control. "There is a secondary fate," he writes, "that attends upon the Actions of persons in this World, and tho we are not able to penitrate into the mysteries of it, or indeed to give any true, and just reasons why things happen so and so, and therefore we call it accident, and fortune; yet we may believe, that we are guided by the influence of our stars, or by the invisible hand of our genius, which so orders the little affairs of every person, according to their good or evil inclinations, and that is it we call opportunity."[9] Whatever meaning may be drawn from this, it is clear that just as the courts of law came to focus more and more on facts and evidence, so fiction came to function in a world of secondary causes and events.

Just as Mary Pix introduced a bit of prose fiction into her comedy, so it is obvious that some of the adventures of Judirina are influenced by the cuckolding plays of the 1670s. The mention of "Lymberhams of the middle size," in one of Judirina's adventures is a direct reference of Dryden's comic portrayal of "keeping" mistresses, and the seduction of Judirina and her subsequent relationship with her first two lovers owes much to this form.[10] But the "Dutch" quality of the story, a reference to its crude realism, moves it from an exemplary tale of sin to the picaresque mode, for though we are given a vivid picture of Judirina in her degraded state, the "subversive" thrust of the story, to use Ronald Paulson's term, is reminiscent of Richard Head and Francis Kirkman's *The English Rogue* with its glorification of the clever, lawless actions of its "extravagant" heroes and heroines.[11]

The line between real events and realistic fictions as well as the problems of taxonomy were often obscure and classification in each group was difficult. Genuine trials and criminal biographies might have been expected to aim at some standard of accuracy, but that was not always the case. *The Lives of Sundry Notorious Villains* (1678) begins with some factual accounts of real criminals and concludes with a novella. To add to the confusion, the novella is advertised on the title page as a true story ("as it really happened at Roan France"). After all, not every crime was given the benefit of a printed narrative. Those that were hawked about the streets were likely to excel in violence and horror; some were selected because they contained a good story, because they had excellent narrative qualities. Occasionally the narrators of these pieces assumed a particular stance. Often they were involved in the narrative as a sympathetic witness to the crime, and occasionally they assumed the ironic, detached stance that Fielding brought to perfection in his *History of the Life of the Late Mr. Jonathan Wild the Great*.

The first systematic collection of criminal accounts to be published in England was Captain Alexander Smith's *History of the Lives and Robberies of the Most Notorious Highwaymen* (1714), which, in its third edition of 1719, was considerably expanded in size and scope. Sale catalogues reveal that many libraries contained the English translation of Alexander Exquemelin's *History of the Buccaneers of America* (1678; first England translation 1684–85), and since English pirates are the substance of Exquemelin's account, it might seem that he ought to be given priority. But Exquemelin was concerned only with piracy. Functioning as a historian, he gave a sustained and detailed account of the raids of Henry Morgan and his followers. Smith, on the other hand, specialized in the brief account of the criminal's life, trial, and end—the pattern to be that of the Newgate Calendar.

Unlikely as it was that such a work would cause commentary at a time when there was no systematic organ for reviewing in England, it did provoke a few remarks from Defoe in the *Weekly Journal*. Embarking on an account of Robert Knight, the villainous, swindling Cashier of the South Sea Company, Defoe remarked that what we sometimes call "white collar crime," and which Foucault calls the "illegality of rights," deserved its historians as well as the deeds of those more honest robbers of the road. Indeed Foucault has shown that the rise of this kind of bourgeois crime was a problem for the legal code of the eighteenth century.[12] Although Defoe's attempt to adapt Smith's biographical model for his brief sketch of Knight was intended to be ironic, his praise for Smith's ingenuity and industry was without apparent undertones of humor. They were worlds apart as writers, but Defoe may well have appreciated the possibilities that Smith opened for him as a writer of criminal fiction and criminal biography.

The tone of the first attempt at a thorough Newgate Calendar was different from that of the most popular and enduring of the series, the nineteenth-century collections of Andrew Knapp and William Baldwin. The type of factual information that Knapp and Baldwin tried to provide was usually absent from Smith's Collection. In addition to the lack of such statistical details, surely crucial in any work purporting to be a historical record, Smith's work differed from its literary offspring in its strange, uneven mixture of occasional irony, fictitious speeches in the manner of classical historians, moralizing, religious reflection, and outright buffoonery that seems to have been drawn from the jestbook tradition. At one point he halts his parade of malefactors to Tyburn for a "character" of England's most notorious prison:

Newgate, which dismal prison is enough to deter all men from acting an ill thing, if they would but consider that it is a place of calamity, a dwelling in more than Cimmerian darkness, an habitation of misery, a confused Chaos without any distinction, a bottomless pit of violence, and a tower of Babel, where all are speakers and no hearers. There is mingling the noble with the ignoble, the rich with the poor, the wise with the ignorant, and debtors with the worst of malefactors. It is the grave of gentility, the banishment of courtesy, the poison of honour, the centre of infamy.[13]

Smith tells stories—fictions stolen from a variety of sources including Boccaccio's *Decameron;* then he makes a turnabout to attack storytelling as evil:

I have no great inclination to tell stories, which perhaps is nothing but the effect of an ill-grounded vanity, that makes me prefer the expressing of what I imagine to the reciting of what I have seen. The profession of a story-teller sits but awkwardly upon young people, and is downright weakness in old men; when our wit is not arrived to its due vigour or when it begins to decline, we then take a pleasure in telling what does not put us to any great expense of thought.[14]

In spite of a few sermons against crime, he regards those who are hanged at Tyburn with a mixture of wonder and genuine awe.

The set speeches are sometimes angry outbursts against the victims of the crime and the society they represent, sometimes general orations on a theme. An example of the first may be found in Smith's account of Bob Congden's reaction to the plea of poverty offered by the chambermaid of the Duchess of Marlborough when he was about to rob her: "You whining bitch, how you throw your snot and snivel about now for nothing at all! Why, so long as you are, by your place, your ladys she-secretary and keep in your custody the box of her teeth, her hair, her patches, and her paint, you'll soon make up your loss again."[15] But Nicholas Horner's discourse on money is more generalized:

I follow the general way of the world, sir, which now prefers money before friends or honesty; yea, some before the salvation of their souls. For it is the love of this that makes an unjust judge to take a bribe, the corrupted lawyer to plead a wrong cause, the physician to kill a man without fear of hanging, and the surgeon to prolong a cure. 'Tis this that makes the tradesman to tell a lie in selling his own ware, the butcher to blow his veal, the tailer to covet so much cabbage, the miller to take toll twice, the baker to wear a wooden cravat, the shoemaker to stretch his leather, as he doth his conscience, and the gentlemen . . . as I am, to wear a Tyburn tippet, or old Storey's cap on some country gallows, which all of our noble profession no more value than you, sir, do the losing of this small trifle of six guineas.[16]

Smith follows this speech with the information that Horner was hanged on 3 April 1719 in his thirty-second year.

Unsure of himself, his audience, and his goals, Smith holds to the notion that straight criminal biography becomes tedious when extended beyond a dozen or so pages and that without a variety of diverting stories and anecdotes the author of them has no hope of holding his readers' attention. Sustained analysis of character and motivation seems to have been beyond his abilities. He did little more than extend the occasional collection of a few individual accounts to a catalogue of criminals covering a number of decades and hundreds of pages. Yet it was more of an accomplishment than might be supposed. By exploiting the variety of criminal activities and providing a panoramic cast of characters, he opened the way for writers of greater talent.

When Defoe praised Smith, he did it precisely in those terms, not so much for his actual achievements as for showing the way to writers interested in exploiting, in a more serious fashion, those ironies that he had barely sketched. When Smith published the third edition of his work, the boom that was to become the South Sea Bubble had just started. The possibility that a group of businessmen might bring financial chaos on a nation seemed confined to the mythical entrepreneur of mercantile ideology who might, through his greed and self-interest, import goods from plague-ridden nations and thereby infect his countrymen. That a plague of dishonesty could have such a wide effect seemed unlikely before the wave of mass speculation caused by the activities of the South Sea Company. Compared to the despair produced by the directors of that Company, the robberies of hungry and desperate men and women seemed almost heroic.

Defoe speculated on the possibilities of an entire collection of lives of this new type of criminal in the manner of his life of Robert Knight:

But before I go any further, I must pay my Acknowledgments to the industrious Captain *Smith* from whose ingenious Volumes of the Lives of Highwaymen, Thieves, Pick-pockets, Cuckolds, and W—— I frankly own I took the design of this Work; him I confess to be my Master in Biography, and entreat the Criticks not to set us together by the Ears: If I excell him, let them consider that he was the Inventor of this Manner of Writing, I only the improver, he wrote only the lives of little Rogues, I of great ones: He had only the Records of the *Old* Bailey and Newgate, I had those of both Houses to collect the Materials for my History from: He has however this Advantage over me, that his Heroes are generally Men of better Spirit, gentiler Education, greater Courage, nobler Endowments, and very often, much better descended than mine.[17]

Several numbers later, a letter was printed in this same journal sympathizing with a poor thief, who had been forced to steal out of "Despair and Hunger" and arguing that the South Sea Bubble had a direct influence on an increase in crime.

This connection became even more explicit in a famous criminal case of 1722, *The Tryal and Condemnation of Arundel Coke*. Coke attempted to enlist the help of a man named Carter in a murder plot against Edward Crispe. According to the testimony, when Carter told Coke that "Scruple of Conscience" would prevent his murdering anyone, Coke urged the greater crimes of the Directors as an excuse for private crimes: "Sir, said I, you mean the *South*-Sea Gentlemen. Yes, said he, so I do; they have ruined Families, and beggar'd Gentlmen: To cut Mens Heads off is but a Trifle to them. Said I, Mr. *Coke*, I believe you speak only in joke, by way of merriment. Said he, What, do you think I sent for you by way of joke? I told him, I could not do any such thing."[18] The dialogue sounds a little like Defoe, and Defoe built similar speculations into his *History of the Pirates* (1724–28).[19] That all of Defoe's criminal narratives, at least all of them written after the period of insane financial speculation, have the comparison between upper-class and lower-class crime as an implicit theme hardly needs arguing in view of his concern with and warnings against the manipulators of Exchange Alley.

What is more to my purpose here, however, is the meeting of fiction and actual life. As we know, Defoe introduced an ideal fictional pirate and a fictionalized real pirate into his study of piracy in order to make certain points about the distinctions between practical problems in colonialism and utopian schemes that were doomed from the start. The popular and frequently reprinted *History of the Pirates* carried such a vision down through the centuries as a form of mythicized history. No work on piracy has contained such firsthand information, but parts of it are essentially fictional in both the creation of character and the recounting of events. As the introduction suggests, many states rose from a collection of thieves to respectability among the nations of the world. Throughout the *History of the Pirates*, Defoe insists on viewing every pirate ship as a potential community and every pirate as a potential social bandit.

Objectivity in history may be neither attainable nor desirable, but the difference between mythic history and an effort at putting together a factual record is considerable, and the division that occurred in the Newgate Calendar provides ample evidence of the distinction. One branch attempted to relate entertaining stories of thieves and their adventures. Published as *The Lives and Adventures of the Most Noted Highwaymen, Pirates, Housebreakers, Street-Robbers,* etc., and under Defoe's old pseudonym, Captain Charles Johnson, in 1734, this collection is dominated by abridged versions of Defoe's lives of pirates and criminals like Jonathan Wild and Jack Shepherd. These criminals, who exerted such a wide fascination for readers in the 1720s, appear alongside such mythic figures as Robin Hood, Falstaff, and Claude du Vall, the gallant thief. And among such desperados, some real, some with but a shadowy reality, appears Defoe's fictional *Colonel Jack.* In this abridgment of Defoe's novel, the complexities of Defoe's almost sentimental beggar boy, thief, plantation owner, and soldier disappear leaving only the myth. But there is enough to suggest that art may shape life.[20] (After all, the broadside ballad of *Moll Flanders* helps inspire Hogarth's Idle Apprentice to a career in crime.) As I will try to show, the presence of Colonel Jack in this frequently reprinted collection is less an indication that Defoe imitated criminal narratives than that the way criminal narratives and criminal behavior were perceived was influenced by Defoe's shaping of them.

Like the mythic Newgate Calendar, the more factual version, developed along the lines of Smith's work, was brought together in 1734. To say that this rendition was a simple accounting of facts and events and a complete contrast to that produced by "Captain Johnson" would be true only to a degree. Certainly there was some emphasis on accuracy; the dates of the crime, trial, and punishment are mentioned in most accounts. But the narratives selected reveal a bias toward the sensational, and there was some effort at presenting a variety of crimes, not merely the account of the ordinary highwayman told over and over again but riots, rapes, and murders. As we shall see, such a tendency to expand the range of criminal acts deserving a place in the Newgate Calendar also extended its possibility as a source and model for realistic fiction. Not only were there a variety of interesting plots, situations, and characters but the people involved were usually those not found in histories of reigns and battles. Before the Newgate Calendars their stories would have been lost in the newspapers and ephemeral broadsides. Now they found a more or less permanent depository for the use of writers exploiting the growing fascination for tales of private, domestic tragedies.

II

Similar accounts were published in the many collections of trials that appeared during the eighteenth and nineteenth centuries. Often the Newgate Calendars and collections of trials covered the same cases, but there were significant differences. The trials had greater status, since they would be seen as examples of the legal system in action.[21] Nevertheless, if sale catalogs are any indication, their popularity went far beyond what would have been expected for legal documents. And those trials that were sold separately and that seem to have had the greatest appeal were the ones with the maximum of dramatic possibilities—sinister poisonings, outrageous acts of cruelty, political trials in which the defendants stood their ground against the oppressive persecution of a government trying to subvert justice. After the success of the first thorough collection of State Trials in 1719, criminal lives, the proper material of the Newgate Calendar, were often sold under the trial's rubric.

From a formal standpoint, the difference between the two ought to have been equivalent to that between the novel and the drama. Trials often gave a brief biographical sketch of the accused party, an account of the crime itself, and some brief relation of the execution or acquittal, but the largest part was devoted to testimony and cross-examination of witnesses for or against the defendant. Both forms of the Newgate Calendar emphasized character and narrative. Testimony was usually reduced to a brief, narrative summary of the arguments.

But if the analogy with the drama and novel is generally correct, the trials still have the type of concentration that would appeal to the novelist, particularly the historical novelist. Accounts of the trials connected with the poisoning of Sir Thomas Overbury were among the most popular. The case contained everything that a novelist might desire—sex in the form of a divorce for impotence, followed by murder and punishment. Ironically enough, the punishment was not for those most guilty but for those who followed orders; the Count and Countess of Somerset, who should have received the heaviest penalties, were pardoned. Also popular was the trial of Sir Francis Bacon with his confession to accepting bribes and his admission to having succumbed to his covetousness. The somber judgment on his death in relative poverty was that "His honour" had died before him.

Who made such a comment? The answer is the editor or writer, perhaps more than one, who gave a particular shape to the trial in the State Trial collections, for as factual as the accounts were, they did have someone to put the material into a particular shape and to moralize about justice.[22] The great gathering of *State Trials*, which ran to eight folio volumes in the edition of 1730–1735, showed more range than the collective versions of the Newgate Calendar, probably because so much might be included under the general heading. The trials were not political in any narrow sense and anything that involved broad legal and social principles found a place. Such catholic representation lends the collection the quality of an impartial history in which the narrator balances the worth of all sides and attempts to see from different angles. Admittedly there are more of the great and powerful than the humble, but some of the poor do make their appearance. And the presence of the trials of Stafford, Laud, and Charles I alongside those of Hampden and other enemies of the court adds to the impression of fairmindedness.

To read the collection in this way would be to project on it a formal organization that, of course, it did not have. The trials provide a cast for a historical novel with characters from the top and bottom of the social ladder, and there are also wonderfully dramatic situations. The reader looking for trials in which innocence was finally vindicated could turn to that of Francia, the Jew, accused of treason by the government but found innocent by the jury, or of the journalist, John Tutchin, prosecuted by the government for libel and barely escaping on technical errors. Few libraries were without the trial of Sacheverell whose violent diatribes against the Dissenters gave him only a small following until the government decided to prosecute him and turned him into a hero. In spite of a lack of unity, then, the State Trials are at the very least an anthology of exciting narratives with a wide appeal to contemporary readers.

As I mentioned above, some of these possibilities were discussed in an abridgment of the State Trials by an editor who claimed to be responsible for the original collection. He pointed to the success of the volumes as a reason for improving them and making them more interesting reading. He argued that more narrative summary was needed. A full trial might include thirty-five challenges, all of which could be collapsed into a single statement giving the number of challenges. "I appeal to any Gentleman who has read a Tryal," he wrote, "if these Repetitions in Print do not create a Weariness and Disgust, and induce him to turn over many Pages unread, whereby perhaps he slips some things that might very well deserve his attention."[23] The editor is not speaking of legal points but rather moments in the narrative that would be of particular enjoyment for a general reader.

If readers did not find politics intriguing, there were sufficient domestic situations for anyone. There was the trial of Lord Audley for voyeurism and sodomy in 1631 or the scandalous relations between Lady Henrieta Berkeley and Lord Grey in 1682 involving a father who could not accept the fact that his daughter was overcome by an irrepressible passion. Cases of servants murdered by their master were common and made rich material for Defoe when he came to select narratives for *The Great Law of Subordination Considered* in 1724. One of the most popular trials was that of Mary Goodenough who murdered her own child for reasons never entirely clear to anyone.

Although the criminals and the witnesses against them are usually the key figures in these trials, the attorneys also emerge as important figures as does the judge, whose attitudes toward defendants and instructions to the jury were anything but impartial. For example, at the trial of Algernon Sidney, Jeffreys, the most outrageous of these judges, constantly warned the defendant against insisting on his "Rights":

Pray don't go away with that Right of mankind, that it is lawful for me to write what I will in my own Closet, unless I publish it: I have been told,

Curse not the King, not in thy Thoughts, not in thy Bed-Chamber, the Birds of the Air will carry it. . . . We must not endure Men to talk, that by the Right of Nature every Man may contrive Mischief in his own Chamber, and he is not to be punished, till he thinks fit to be called to it.[24]

The Justices of the Peace, who appear in Fielding's *Joseph Andrews* and in Godwin's *Caleb Williams*, are exaggerated, satirical portraits only to a degree. An impartial system of justice was utopian speculation. No wonder, then, that Caleb Williams has to renounce any reliance on it—any belief that through it he might have his innocence vindicated—before he is able to achieve a moral stance above that of his enemy, Falkland, whose manipulation of the system corrupts his very soul.

The rendering of court scenes in fiction is a large enough subject for separate treatment. What I am involved with in this paper is its part in the entire system of relationships between the real event and its rendering. Fielding, of course, staged his hearings as minidramas, but most novelists tended to locate the most important aspects of the trial experience in the minds of those present. Most importantly, the trials taught novelists that however much they might improve them by abridgment and proper editing, they could not speculate on what might have been going on in the minds of the parties involved without indulging in a form of fiction. At the same time, they showed that there was a reading public that did not have to be amused by comic pieces, an audience that was fascinated by a situation involving life and death and turning on points of guilt and innocence. Because the trials were considerably longer than the usual Newgate Calendar entry, they also showed that interest in such subjects might be sustained for hundreds of pages. Even the Newgate Calendar began to give more pages over to trials of particular interest, sometimes providing the psychological analysis that was beyond the scope of the trials.

III

Although some criminal lives are deliberate fictions and others approach fictions because of an inadequate sense of historical truth on the part of the writer, there is a more subtle pressure exerted by fiction on the Newgate Calendar. At a time when the line between fiction and history was even more ambiguous than it is today, works of fiction often functioned as "true histories" and began to shape patterns of behavior and daydreams. For example, it hardly seems conceivable that Lord Baltimore's rape of Miss Woodcock, which continued to occupy an unusual number of pages in these collections into the nineteenth century, would have received much attention if Richardson had not exploited similar events in *Pamela, Clarissa,* and *Grandison.* The case of Lord Baltimore did not follow the usual pattern of violent crime followed by violent punishment. Knapp and Baldwin confess that neither Lord Baltimore nor any of his accomplices were ever punished but maintain that "although conviction did not follow the trials of these presumed offenders, it is our duty to state the affair as it was transmitted to the public at that time."[25] Why they feel that this case demanded telling more than others is not explained beyond this comment, but the parallel with Richardson's fictional accounts should be obvious enough.

The narrative is centered on the ways in which wealth and power may be used to destroy innocence, and in the Knapp-Baldwin version of the Newgate Calendar it is accompanied by an illustration that makes Lord Baltimore look like Volpone acting a somewhat similar role, while his female assistants, graphic versions of Richardson's Jewkes and Sinclair, bring Miss Woodcock to his bed. The events themselves seem familiar. Miss Woodcock is tricked into a coach and taken to a house. She cries out for help from a window but is forced inside. She begs for her liberty and resists Lord Baltimore's advances. After six unsuccessful attempts on her chastity in two hours, Lord Baltimore decides to use drugs to render her unconscious. He rapes her then in much the same way as, though with far less patience than, Lovelace rapes Clarissa. Fearing that her mysterious rapist, whose identity she now discovers, may try to pass her on to his servants, Miss Woodcock tries even more desperately to escape. She is finally rescued by Sir John Fielding and taken away from her captors.

How many hints Lord Baltimore may have taken from Squire B——, Lovelace, and Sir Hargrave is difficult to say. Indeed he probably didn't need any. But the writers of the account reveal an awareness of the ways in which the libertine nobility preyed on innocent victims among the middle and lower orders that would have been impossible before Richardson's renditions of this time. Among Richardson's seducers, Lord Baltimore appears most like Sir Hargrave, but as in *Clarissa*, there is neither a change of mind nor of heart on the part of the seducer. Neither is there a successful rescue. The verdict of not guilty returned by the jury on the twenty-sixth of March 1768 sounds like the script written by Lovelace in that wonderful daydream of justification and vindication that follows his fantasy of throwing Hickman into the sea and sailing off the coast of France while he and his gang take turns raping Miss Howe and her mother.[26] I think that in this instance, then, we can be fairly certain that fiction conditioned both the selection of the case and the attitude toward the crime. If it also influenced Lord Baltimore's daydreams, then we can speculate that while most modern critics have been struck by the first part of Ian Watt's formula for seduction scenes in Richardson as "sermon and striptease," readers like Lord Baltimore may have been more fascinated by the undressing.[27]

Yet what gets the vote for being the "most remarkable and extraordinary trial in our whole Calendar," as one collection calls it, is not this rape nor any of the violent and sensational murders, but rather the case of Eugene Aram, rightly described as "the topic of general conversation, and the subject of every pen."[28] The reason for the popularity of this case has nothing to do with its importance as setting legal precedents, and while separate publications are often called the "trial" of Eugene Aram, the interest is always in the pattern of his actions, thoughts, and passions. And as a criminal life, the major concern is novelistic in the sense that the plot involves a direct connection between a past life and a present one, between cause and effect and between action and retribution.

The story was and still is well known. Burdened by debts and married to a woman whom he had grown to hate, Eugene Aram, a schoolteacher at Knaresborough, began to engage in shady dealings with some of his fellow townsmen, including the victim, Daniel Clark. After a dispute over money, Aram, along with a fellow criminal, Houseman, murdered Clark, buried the body, and disappeared. Thirteen years later the body, or rather a skeleton, was discovered. Houseman confessed to seeing Aram strike Clark, and the authorities proceeded to arrest Aram in Lynn, where he had achieved respectability and some prominence as a scholar and master of many languages, including Celtic. Although he pointed to the nature of his recent life as evidence of his innocence, he was found guilty and, after an unsuccessful attempt at suicide, hanged. His body was taken to Knaresborough forest and put in chains, and the story is still Knaresborough's chief claim to fame in the *Blue Guide*.

Although the case of Eugene Aram always receives what appears to be a disproportionately large amount of space in the Newgate Calendars, there it is made to conform to the general format of the criminal life. But *The Genuine Account of the Trial of Eugene Aram for the Murder of Daniel Clark,* one of the many separate publications on the case, and in its tenth edition by 1810, is as good an example of the separate criminal biography as that form passed from the eighteenth to the nineteenth century. From what we have seen previously, it is hardly surprising that the work is not a "trial" at all but rather a compendium of genres and subgenres that had come together to form the standard criminal life. The same processes had been at work with literary biographies, which had come to incorporate letters, conversations, and documents in the chronological narrative. Hence *The Genuine Account* contains such miscellaneous items as the report on the discovery of the skeleton, Aram's original statement of his innocence containing a list of accused criminals whose innocence had been discovered only after they had already been executed, an autobiographical account of his process in studying languages, a report of a confession he had made before two clergymen, and collections of his writings—from pieces on Celtic as the language from which English came to some poems and a defence of suicide. The author-editor moves from analysis of the evidence, such as his observations that Aram did not know of Houseman's confession when he wrote his original defence, to an account of the execution. He concludes with some moral judgments on the nature of Aram's criminality, observing that he had progressed from the relatively minor offense of stealing and selling plants from gardens in the neighborhood to the terrible crime of murder.

The appeal of this narrative should be apparent enough. In addition to the satisfying theme that murder will out no matter how well concealed, the story raised some perplexing ethical problems. Since Eugene Aram lived a moral and productive life during the thirteen years following the murder, should he be convicted for a crime that he committed when he was, in some sense, a different person?[29] Cases like that of Eugene Aram raise questions about the nature of crime and punishment and create that type of ambiguity perfect for the production of fiction. The idea runs through novels as diverse as *Colonel Jack*, *Les Miserables*, and *The Mayor of Casterbridge*. Like these fictions, Aram's story does not achieve tragic dimensions. Even less than the heroes of these works, he fails to demonstrate either sufficient moral stature or social status. Aram's father had been a "master" gardener, but he still labored with his hands. As a scholar, Aram showed some ability, however, and when arrested he had gained a degree of respectability. Indeed, some of the fascination with Aram's crime may reside in the notion that even learned men may become criminals; some may lie with the hint of violent passions at work in the presence of a wife whom he blamed for having driven him to crime. But the most compelling aspect of the story of this man who raised himself by his own talents and industry is the hint of what Alexander Welsh has argued lies behind all such stories—not tragedy but the hint of a cosmic practical joke.[30]

That the story of Eugene Aram was not turned into a novel before Bulwer's effort in 1831 is almost as surprising as the weakness of his rendering of such rich material. A novelistic account of Aram's life must have been tempting to Bulwer after the success of his first Newgate novel, *Paul Clifford* (1830), but the decision to sentimentalize the story was unfortunate. He has Aram confess that he hoped to use the money to do good for mankind and turns Clark, a violent man who deserts his wife and child, rapes a girl, and forces her to commit suicide, into a candidate for murder by any passing humanitarian. Even transforming the murder into a noble action is insufficient for Bulwer. He stresses the virtues of Aram in portraying his love for his daughter and his sufferings in being blackmailed by Houseman. Finally, Bulwer changes him into an accomplice in the murder rather than the main agent.

Bulwer's failure says much about the swerve from a realistic rendering of crime in, for example, Defoe toward a genteel type of novel that placed a heavy emphasis on the idealized love plot. When Bulwer comes to describe London's slums with its prostitutes, he apologizes profusely and moralizes unbearably. He even feels it necessary to apologize to his readers for having to mention money, explaining that in "writing a romance of real life" an author had to include such unsavory details. The very popularity of Bulwer's work demonstrated how well he knew his audience. The materials of life were still available in the Newgate Calendar, but the kind of transformation of such materials to realistic fiction or even to the detailed picture of evil in Gothic fiction was becoming more difficult at a time when romance had so powerfully reasserted itself. Readers also wanted more psychological interpretation than the criminal biographies provided, but Bulwer gave them easy, stereotypical motivation in place of real insight. And the same may be said for his moralizing. He placed a footnote near the end of his work in which he argued that Aram's attempt at suicide shows a lack of Christian fortitude. Without quarreling with Bulwer's novel in the way that Bulwer quarreled with his material, I would simply suggest that other novelists had better success in drawing from trials and criminal biographies.

William Godwin's *Caleb Williams* takes ideas from a number of lives in the Newgate Calendar, but like so many readers, he was attracted to the story of Eugene Aram and the notion of a person pursued by a past crime. He probably took some hints from Defoe's *Roxana*, but the episode in which Caleb establishes himself in a Welsh village as a watchmaker, devoting himself to the study of the etymology of languages, is taken directly from the life of Aram. And in the context of the work itself as well as in Godwin's *Political Justice* can be perceived the possibility of a different end for a man like Eugene Aram than the revenge of a meaningless system of justice.

The tendency of critics to make an almost automatic leap from the ambiguities of *Caleb Williams* to the ideological explanations of *Political Justice* may have prevented them from seeing just how much of a Newgate novel Godwin wrote. Caleb's initial crime is merely an act of curiosity, something far less violent than that of Eugene Aram but equally capable of destroying the social bond. Like a number of figures in the Newgate Calendar, he is a victim of persecution in spite of his innocence. Even the disguises he assumes, particularly that of the Jew, has its echoes in a number of Jewish criminals who manage to enter the Calendar toward the end of the eighteenth century. And of course Godwin draws directly on Defoe's fictional section of *The History of the Pirates*, "Of Captain Misson," in portraying his bandit leader, Captain Raymond. Just as Captain Misson raised the flag of liberty in a world that forced the poor and enslaved to "dance to the Musick of their Chains," so Captain Raymond proclaims that the thieves of his gang follow the "profession of justice," in a society that distorts the very idea of justice.[31]

Caleb rejects Raymond's war on society, though his own notion of justice at this point in the novel is probably less realistic than that of the bandit leader. The crucial point, however, is that Godwin's use of the Newgate Calendar was highly imaginative and creative. He saw in this series of lives not only a fascinating group of narratives but a catalog of wrongs on both sides of the law—wrongs shocking enough to condemn the entire machinery of justice. It was not the creation of a wholly new psychological fiction from this material that made Godwin original; Defoe had done much the same in *Roxana* and in parts of *Moll Flanders* and *Colonel Jack*. And Defoe had also used various legal ideologies—natural law, religious law—to challenge the traditional readings of justice. But Godwin saw in the lives of criminals proof that true justice played no part in these bloody and violent careers. To read the Newgate Calendar was to experience vivid evidence of the breakdown of humane relationships in contemporary society.

An artful touch in this regard comes when Caleb is hunted out of Wales by the publication and distribution of a typical criminal biography of Caleb. That the facts are false and the publication merely a weapon against Caleb aimed at him by his enemy Falkland suggests that the historical record of crime is distorted by the poisoned system producing it. Godwin's ideological bias is both a strength and a weakness. It gives intellectual force to the strange series of punishments visited on Caleb after he surrenders to his curiosity about his master, searches through his papers during a fire, and thereby incurs his wrath. But the ambiguities arising from Caleb's situation are not entirely novelistic; behind them lie the kinds of definite answers and solutions that Godwin explored in *Political Justice*. What keeps the novel strong and prevents it from becoming too abstract are those scenes of jails and the suffering inmates, of courts and of the underworld—scenes that directly reflect the realism of the Newgate Calendar. And Godwin's realism was a direct product of the Newgate Calendar.

IV

Until now I have been treating works involving the individual criminal or a small group, and how much influence such figures had on the novel has already been implied. The genuine criminal violence present in *Clarissa*, for example, is considerable. Mowbray, the least sensible of Lovelace's crew, is an absolute brute, capable of all kinds of cruelty, and Lovelace, for all his pretense at feeling and sensibility, is more sadistic than Lord Baltimore. The kidnapping of Clarissa is a criminal act, and Clarissa's appeal to her rights as a citizen should be taken seriously. The call for true justice has a place in fiction from the earliest times on through Radcliffe's Vivaldi in *The Italian* to Faulkner's *Requiem for a Nun*. But equally important as individual justice and certainly more surprising in the Newgate Calendar are cases involving groups of men accused of participating in riots. Such collective lives or trials have a direct relationship to the historical novel.

The riots were not always overtly political. Sometimes, as with those riots occasioned by the efforts of a London mob to pull down some bawdy houses in March of 1668, the rioters were on the side of traditional morality. Nevertheless they were brought to trial under the charge of making "Public War against Charles II" and found guilty. The Porteus riots, which play a part in Scott's *Heart of Midlothian*, have a place in the Newgate Calendars as do the activities of the Waltham Blacks about whom E. P. Thompson has written so well. The Riot Act of 1715 was intended to suppress the turmoil caused by city mobs, and the Black Acts of 1723 made crimes against property hanging offenses almost automatically. Such laws seemed to have been ineffective in discouraging the activities of mobs, as the many studies of George Rudé have demonstrated.[32] Perhaps the reason for the failure of the laws was the underlying awareness on both sides—the authorities and the turbulent mobs—that the riots were social and economic in their origins. For example, James Murphy and John Dogan were executed after a riot nominally associated with the demagogue, John Wilkes, but that was clearly connected with labor unrest. Some of those accused seemed to have been present at the riots merely by chance, and the very refusal of the prosecution to make exceptions gave a kind of pathos to these trials that would appeal to any novelist.[33]

Since mobs were composed of the poor, apprentices, and artisans, the possibilities inherent in such material were available only to those writers who did not think of fiction exclusively in terms of romance with a cast of noble characters. As might have been expected, Defoe was capable of treating this subject, and as I have shown elsewhere, his central concern in A Journal of the Plague Year was with order and disorder in a time of extremity rather than with a historical account of the sickness.[34] But the major upheaval of the century for Great Britain came in 1780 under the influence of Lord George Gordon. Although all the newspapers and many pamphleteers recorded the devastation caused by the mobs, the Newgate Calendar recorded these events in more or less permanent form. Riots were criminal acts, and the compilers of Newgate Calendars found in the Gordon Riots mass criminality on a scale that nothing in the annals of history could match. One of the editors commented:

We must here observe that the enormous outrages committed by these abandoned wretches were so numerous and terrifying, and the further mischiefs dreaded from their menaces were so tremendous, that (as we remarked of one of the cruel Roman emperors) one would almost think that Divine Providence had suffered them to run to such shocking lengths to shew what horrid excesses the human mind is capable of when left to its own evil bias without restraint.[35]

The best novel to concentrate on these riots and perhaps on riots of any kind is Dickens's Barnaby Rudge, and while Dickens's overall use of the Newgate Calendar is a large subject and beyond the scope of this book, I want to use this one novel to make a few remarks on the historical novel.

By far the best and certainly the most influential work on this form is by Georg Lukács, who interprets it in terms of mass action and popular turmoil.[36] Dickens wrote of such movements from the standpoint of the bourgeoisie, which was similar to the way Knapp and Baldwin presented them in the Newgate Calendar. Popular insurrection was seen in terms of mass criminality and the destruction of property was made almost synonymous with the destruction of a life. Dickens views London during the time of the Gordon Riots as a city dominated by criminals with the suggestion that society, at least modern society, must fall into chaos when there is no effective police force to control the mob. Dickens portrays the leaders of the mob, individually, as criminals, and the force of this statement is not diminished by the presence of an agent of the law—the hangman—among them, for in its practical working out of punishment, the law is likely to be imperfect. In the larger fiction, the riots seem to be a projection of individual violence—the unrevenged murder of Reuben Haredale by his servant twenty-seven years earlier. In burning down the Warren, the house in which the murder occurred, twenty of the arsonists die. Shortly thereafter the murderer is caught and the taint on the property is finally removed. Also removed is the taint of murder itself. Rudge, like Eugene Aram, Falkland, and Roxana, survive the time when they have committed criminal acts, but they are haunted beings—haunted by their horror at their past and their fear that somehow they will be discovered. Rudge, who is thought to be dead, frequently returns to the area of the Warren, frightening all who see him, and never finds relief until all is revealed. The theme that fascinated Defoe from the very beginning and which he included in his *Historical Collections,* had become a central theme in the novel. Dickens used this element of Newgate fiction as a way of giving interest to his private plot, but for the most part, he is concerned with the reflection of private crime in the public act that becomes part of history.

And from the standpoint of history, a comparison between Dickens's novel and Defoe's *Journal of the Plague Year* is instructive. Defoe's three craftsmen struggle across London and out into the countryside, leading a group of citizens who refuse to obey the unjust law that would quarantine the city and deprive them of their right to survive. It partakes of the spirit of revolt that informs the earlier, mythic versions of the Newgate Calendar that Defoe helped to create. Dickens, writing in the spirit of the version produced by Knapp and Baldwin, makes *Barnaby Rudge* into a saga asserting the glories of law and order, and by equating the right to property with the sacredness of the self, he extended the idea to cover everything good in love, home, and the family. Defoe too has his H. F., the Saddler, a responsible Londoner who stays in the city during the plague, partly to protect his property, but he balances this angle of vision against his mutinous artisans. On a number of occasions, Dickens uses the comparison of the mob to a plague on the land. In Defoe, the group led by the three artisans struggle bravely against a plague that would kill them all. The two branches of the Newgate Calendar eventually both conditioned and became part of the social vision of the eighteenth and nineteenth centuries.

I remarked at the start of this discussion that I had no intention of covering the multitude of problems in the relationship between accounts of criminals and criminality. Rather, I have tried to suggest an interaction between some particular forms of realistic narrative, the novel, and the life of the times as rendered through narratives. Of course the violent acts featured in the Newgate Calendar and State Trials influenced a different kind of novel than, say, *Emma*, in which the crimes are personal infringements of a social and ethical code—Frank Churchill's careless treatment of Jane Fairfax and Emma's inconsiderate pattern of thought that finds its way out into the social world in her remarks to Miss Bate at Box Hill. If these "crimes" are typical of those in the novel of manners, even Jane Austen has her Willoughby and Wickham to threaten more violent deeds. And few novelists could resist a story like Eugene Aram in which a past crime would destroy present prosperity. Versions of the tale of the murderer brought suddenly to confess his guilt after many years fascinated Defoe as it did Dickens and Dostoevski. Both Swift and Fielding produced brilliant satire on what they saw as a misplaced infatuation with crime, but they underrated its potential artistic power as they (and many modern critics) underrated Defoe and realistic narrative generally.

Notes

Introduction

1. Theophilus Cibber et al., *The Lives of the Poets*, 5 vols. (London, 1753), 4:325. Most of the work in this collection has been ascribed to Robert Shiels.
2. *Weekly Journal*, (8 November 1718): 1195.
3. For an antagonist's description of Defoe holding forth to a group of disciples, see the piece reprinted in my "A Whiff of Scandal in the Life of Daniel Defoe," *HLQ*, 34 (1970): 35–42.
4. Alexander Pope, *Epilogue to the Satires, Poems*, ed. John Butt et al., 6 vols. (London: Methuen, 1939), 4:324–35.
5. Daniel Defoe, *A Review of the Affairs of France*, ed. Arthur W. Secord, 22 vols. (New York: Columbia, 1938), 1:153.
6. Northrop Frye, *The Anatomy of Criticism* (Princeton: Princeton University Press, 1957), pp. 304–5.

Chapter 1

1. Daniel Defoe, *A Continuation of Letters Written by a Turkish Spy at Paris* (London, 1718), p. iv.
2. Ian Watt, *The Rise of the Novel* (Berkeley: University of California Press, 1957), p. 70.
3. Watt's book provoked a reassessment of Defoe's craftsmanship. David Blewett and Everett Zimmerman have written on Defoe's fictional structures, and James Sutherland and John Richetti have written on the way Defoe explored new states of feeling in creating his fictional characters. See Blewett, *Defoe's Art of Fiction* (Toronto: University of Toronto Press, 1979); Zimmerman, *Defoe and the Novel* (Berkeley: University of California Press, 1975); Sutherland, *Daniel Defoe* (Cambridge, Mass.: Harvard University Press, 1971); and Richetti, *Defoe's Narratives* (Oxford: Clarendon Press, 1975).
4. "Historical Collections," William Andrews Clark Memorial Library MS H6735M3, pp. 126–27.

5. *Review*, ed. Arthur W. Secord (New York: Columbia University Press, 1938), 8:253b.

6. See the Introduction above, pp. xi–xii. John Dunton considered Defoe's *The True-Born Englishman* "the finest piece of Wit that this Age has produced" and praised him for his originality, natural genius, inventiveness, and "clear sense." See Dunton, *Dunton's Whipping Post* (London, 1706), pp. 88–91; and Dunton, *The Life and Errors of John Dunton* (London, 1705), pp. 239–40.

7. Daniel Defoe, *Robinson Crusoe*, ed. J. Donald Crowley (London: Oxford University Press, 1972), p. 118.

8. Richard Head and Francis Kirkman, *The English Rogue* (London, 1680; rptd. 1874), 4:257.

9. Eric Auerbach, *Mimesis* (Garden City: Doubleday, 1957), pp. 3–20.

10. Ralph Fox, *The Novel and the People* (London: Lawrence and Wishard, 1937), pp. 17–46. See also Christopher Caudwell, *Illusion and Reality* (New York: International Publishers, 1963), pp. 262–69.

11. Wayne Booth, *The Rhetoric of Fiction* (Chicago: University of Chicago Press, 1961), pp. 41–42.

12. Northrop Frye, *The Anatomy of Criticism* (Princeton: Princeton University Press, 1957), pp. 303–14.

13. Diana Spearman, *The Novel and Society* (New York: Barnes and Noble, 1966), p. 51.

14. See Watt, *The Rise of the Novel*, pp. 12–21; and my "Defoe's Theory of Fiction," *SP*, 61 (1964): 661–62.

15. See Michael R. Watts, *The Dissenters* (Oxford: Clarendon Press, 1978), 1:370–371; and W. A. L. Vincent, *The Grammar Schools* (London: John Murray, 1969), p. 195.

16. Pat Rogers, *Robinson Crusoe* (London: Allen and Unwin, 1979), p. 53.

17. See René Wellek, *The Contexts of Criticism*, ed. Stephen Nichols, Jr. (New Haven: Yale University Press, 1963), pp. 222–55.

18. See Bernard Weinberg, *French Realism: The Critical Reaction, 1830–1870* (New York: Modern Language Association of America, 1937), especially pp. 119–42, 192–95.

19. Linda Nochlin, *Realism* (Harmondsworth: Pelican Books, 1978), p. 14.

20. Sir Walter Scott, *On Novels and Novelists*, ed. Ioan Williams (New York: Barnes and Noble, 1968), pp. 172–74.

21. Daniel Defoe, *The Storm* (London, 1704), sigs. A4^v–A5.

22. Roland Barthes, "Myth Today," *Mythologies*, trans. Annette Lavars (New York: Hill and Wang, 1972), pp. 109–59.

23. Claude Lévi-Strauss, *The Savage Mind* (London: Weidenfeld and Nicholson, 1962), pp. 217–69. See also Mircea Eliade, *The Sacred and Profane*, trans. Willard Trask (New York: Harcourt, Brace and World, 1959), pp. 68–113.

24. Michael Oakeshott, *Hobbes on Civil Association* (Berkeley: University of California Press, 1975), p. 154. For a somewhat similar view of these systems as creative systems, see Wiley Sypher, *Rococo to Cubism in Art and Literature* (New York: Vintage Books, 1963), p. 19.

25. See Edward Stillingfleet, *Works* (London, 1710), p. 563.

26. Samuel Pufendorf, *An Introduction to the History of the Principal Kingdoms and States of Europe* (London, 1687), p. 1. See also Defoe, *Jure Divino* (London, 1706), bk. 2, p. 4. Although Pufendorf draws upon Genesis, his method is independent of the much criticized use of typology. Defoe, who could, on occasion, employ biblical references with full typological import, would have understood the distinction.

27. Sir Walter Raleigh, *The History of the World* (London, 1687), p. 1.

28. Leonard Krieger, *The Politics of Discretion* (Chicago: University of Chicago Press, 1965), pp. 202–18. That fresh political myths were being manufactured at the same time that a new interest in the pagan myths was spreading is not without significance. See Burton Feldman and Robert Richards, eds., *The Rise of Modern Mythology* (Bloomington: University of Indiana Press, 1972), pp. xx–xxv, 3–92.

29. Ian Watt, "The Recent Critical Fortunes of Moll Flanders," *ECS* 1 (1967): 111, 117.

30. Wilkie Collins, *Works* (New York: Peter Fenelon Collier, n.d.), 6:126 (chap. 10).

31. See Manuel Schonhorn, "Defoe: The Literature of Politics and the Politics of Some Fictions," *English Literature in the Age of Disguise*, ed. Maximillian E. Novak (Berkeley: University of California Press, 1977), p. 24.

32. This is Defoe in the *Master Mercury* of 8 August 1704 commenting on his own journalism in the *Review*.

33. See Joseph Browne, *A Dialogue between Church and No-Church*, in *State Tracts*, 2 vols. (London, 1715), 1:6–35.

34. Samuel Coleridge, *Biographia Literaria*, ed. J. Shawcross, 2 vols. (London: Oxford University Press, 1962). 2:12.

35. An exception is James Walton's "The Romance of Gentility: Defoe's Heroes and Heroines," *Literary Monographs*, ed. Eric Rothstein (Madison: University of Wisconsin Press, 1971), 4:91–135.

36. Daniel Defoe, *Review* 7 (11 April 1710): 25a.

37. See the *Tatler*, nos. 132, 264, 268.

38. See Novak, "Defoe's Theory of Fiction," p. 661.

39. Peter Earle, *The World of Defoe* (New York: Athenaeum, 1977), p. 230.

40. John Robert Moore, *A Checklist of the Writings of Daniel Defoe* (Bloomington: Indiana University Press, 1960), p. 1.

41. Walter Wilson, *Memoirs of the Life and Times of Daniel De Foe*, 3 vols. (London: Hurst, Chance & Co., 1830), 3:645–46.

42. Defoe, "Historical Collections," pp. 63–64.

43. Plutarch, *The Lives of the Noble Grecians and Romans* (London, 1657), p. 364.

44. Apothegms and collections of brief anecdotes were still popular in 1682, though a clear tendency toward some kind of change in the form is apparent. John Bulteel defines the form as "a pithy and short Sentiment upon a Subject; or a ready, and sharp answer, which causeth Laughter, or Admiration." He tried to make his more concise and avoid transforming them into mere stories. On the other hand, William Winstanley, like Defoe, is intrigued by narrative. See John Bulteel, *The Apophthegmes of the Ancients* (London, 1683), sig. A6; and

William Winstanley, *Histories and Observations Domestick and Foreign* (London, 1683), sig. A3.

45. Defoe, "Historical Collections," p. 66.
46. Daniel Defoe, *Memoirs*, ed. John T. Boulton (London: Oxford University Press, 1972), p. 68.
47. Defoe, "Historical Collections," pp. 68–69.
48. See William Lee, *The Life and Newly Discovered Writings of Daniel Defoe*, 3 vols. (London: J. C. Hotten, 1869), 3:110–11; for a possible source, see *The English Rogue*, 4:231.
49. See *The Quarrel of the School-Boys at Athens* (London, 1717) as it was reviewed in Defoe's *Mercurius Politicus*, January 1717, p. 43: "It is most easie to understand the meaning of all this, and indeed the Story is so very unluckily told, that it needs no Application, neither does the Writer of it make any."

Chapter 2

1. Joseph Browne, *A Dialogue between Church and No-church; or, A Rehearsal of the Review* (1706), in *State Tracts* (London, 1715), 1:6, 35.
2. Daniel Defoe, *The Life and Strange Surprising Adventures of Robinson Crusoe*, ed. J. Donald Crowley (London: Oxford University Press, 1972), p. 154. All subsequent references to this work and to *The Farther Adventures of Robinson Crusoe* will be included in parentheses in my text. For the latter work I have used *The Shakespeare Head Edition of Daniel Defoe* (Oxford: Blackwell, 1927).
3. For a source study of *Robinson Crusoe*, see Arthur W. Secord, *Studies in the Narrative Method of Defoe*, University of Illinois Studies in Language and Literature, no. 1 (Urbana: University of Illinois Press, 1924), 9:21–111.
4. Daniel Defoe, the *Master Mercury*, 8 August 1704, p. 3.
5. Gaston Bachelard, *The Poetics of Space*, trans. Maria Jolas (Boston: Beacon Press, 1970), p. 9.
6. Quoted in James T. Hillhouse, *The Grub-Street Journal* (Durham: Duke University Press, 1928), p. 49.
7. It was precisely as "a Translator of the Foreign News" that Defoe introduced himself into Nathaniel Mist's *Weekly Journal* and under that disguise gained enough control of its Tory policies to "prevent the Mischievous Part of it." *The Letters of Daniel Defoe*, ed. George H. Healey (Oxford: Clarendon Press, 1955), p. 453.
8. See for example J. Read's *Weekly Journal*, 1 November 1718, p. 1191. Read printed a series of poems in the next few issues revealing Defoe as a satanic forger of lies.
9. *Weekly Journal*, 22 November 1718, p. 607.
10. *Daniel Defoe: His Life and Recently Discovered Writings*, ed. William Lee, 3 vols. (London: John Hotten, 1869), vols. 2 and 3.
11. *Weekly Journal*, 7 February 1719, p. 56.
12. I argued this point in my *Economics and the Fiction of Daniel Defoe* (Berkeley: University of California Press, 1962), p. 36, but I did not give the evidence for

my conclusion. Defoe had nothing to do with titles describing how he "colo-
nised" the island, but it is far from being an invention of modern com-
mentators.

13. Bachelard, *Poetics of Space*, p. 32.

14. See *Mercurius Politicus*, February 1718, p. 101, for a discussion of the way in
which the lack of small coins would cripple commerce. In *Weekly Journal* he
told the story of Tom Pickaxe whose family had to go hungry because no
tradesman would give him change for a guinea. See the issue of 18 January
1718, pp. 343–44, for this and other comments on the coinage.

15. See Healey, *Letters*, p. 474.

16. *Mercurius Politicus*, January 1718, p. 5.

17. Ibid., March 1718, p. 199.

18. Ibid., April 1718, p. 258.

19. *Weekly Journal*, 2 August 1718, p. 509.

20. Ibid., 9 August 1718, p. 515. The *"certain writer"* is Defoe himself. For an
analogy with English affairs, see ibid., 22 March 1718, p. 401.

21. See ibid., 1 March 1718; and *Mercurius Britannicus*, March 1718, p. 129.

22. *Robinson Crusoe,* pp. 68–69: "So that had my Cave been to be seen, it look'd
like a general Magazine of all Necessary things, and I had every thing so ready
at my Hand, that it was a great Pleasure to me to see all my Goods in such
Order, and especially to find my Stock of all Necessaries so great."

23. In fact he can be impatient with writers who attribute all storms to God's or
Satan's wrath. See for example his remark on wrecks in the Orkneys in *A Tour
thro' the Whole Island of Great Britain*, 2 vols. (London: Peter Davies, 1927),
2:824.

24. Mrs. Radcliffe's novels depicting scenes of disaster at sea dwell on the fascination and half pleasure felt by the viewer. Such a scene also sets Crusoe's
imagination working, but Defoe does not exploit the feeling of pleasure from
viewing the distress of others from a safe vantage point. See *Robinson Crusoe,*
1:216–17.

25. *Weekly Journal*, 11 January 1718, p. 330; *Mercurius Politicus,* December 1717, pp.
900, 901, 902.

26. *Mercurius Politicus*, January 1718, p. 59; *Weekly Journal*, 18 January 1718, p. 344.

27. *Weekly Journal*, 19 March 1718, p. 390.

28. G. S. Starr, "Escape from Barbary: A Seventeenth-Century Genre," *HLQ* 29
(1965): 35–52.

29. See *Weekly Journal*, 13 September 1718, p. 548. This was a translation of a novel
by Eustache Le Noble de Tennelière written in 1694. For Defoe's personal
involvement with Moorish pirates, see John Robert Moore, *Daniel Defoe Citizen
of the Modern World* (Chicago: University of Chicago Press, 1958), p. 265.

30. *Mercurius Politicus*, November 1718, p. 696.

31. For the theme of starvation at sea in *Robinson Crusoe,* see p. 139, and p. 187, as
well as the large section in *The Farther Adventures.*

32. E. M. Tillyard, *The Epic Strain in the English Novel* (London: Chatto, 1958), p.
45. For a discussion of anxiety and fiction see Simon Lesser, *Fiction and the
Unconscious* (New York: Vintage, 1962), pp. 254–62.

33. See William Winstanley, *Poor Robin's Visions: Wherein Is Described the Present Humours of the Times* (London, 1677). In Defoe's day *Poor Robin* was the name of an almanac with a "Prognostication" of events toward the end.

34. See, for example, *Mercurius Politicus*, January 1719, pp. 34–37.

35. Ibid., April 1718, pp. 208–9.

36. *Weekly Journal*, 20 September 1718, p. 553. Crusoe says of his plundering his wreck, "I believe verily, had the calm Weather held, I should have brought away the whole Ship Piece by Piece," and we have the feeling in these passages that he is acting more like a superman than the everyman he often pretends to be. For another case of marooning, see *Mercurius Politicus*, February 1719, p. 77.

37. Daniel Defoe, *Serious Reflections of Robinson Crusoe* (London: W. Taylor, 1720), sig. A2ᵛ. Although Defoe tries to draw exact parallels between Crusoe's life and his own, he leaves the suggestion that the work is like his life in a broadly symbolic sense, and I would agree that *Robinson Crusoe* is certainly closer to his imaginative life—his creative daydream life—than are any of his other fictions. See also Angus Fletcher, *Allegory* (Ithaca: Cornell University Press, 1967), pp. 53–54 especially.

38. *Serious Reflections*, p. 3. See also *Robinson Crusoe*, p. 63.

39. *Serious Reflections*, p. 2.

40. Tillyard, *The Epic Strain*, pp. 25–50.

41. Defoe's involvement with the relationship between Presbyterian and Anglican clergymen in Scotland goes back to the time he was in Scotland fighting for the union of the two countries. In 1707 he published an attack on the Anglicans with the ironic title: *An Historical Account of the Bitter Sufferings, and Melancholy Circumstances of the Episcopal Church in Scotland, Under the Barbarous Usage and Bloody Persecution of the Presbyterian Government*. The Jacobite invasion of 1715 revived this interest, and he devoted a number of pamphlets to ways of depriving Jacobite clergymen in Scotland and England of a platform for sedition.

42. Daniel Defoe, *Memoirs of the Church of Scotland* (London, 1717), p. 226.

43. Ibid., p. 235. Crusoe's thoughts when he discovers his grotto (see above, p. 66) may also echo this passage of the Bible.

44. Defoe, *Memoirs of the Church*, p. 231.

45. Ibid., pp. 258–61.

46. In an entry somewhat late for my purpose but expressive of his true attitude, Defoe wrote, "We think that the Protestant Principle, that is *the Bible* is *the only and the perfect Rule of Faith*," and he suggested that the ministers at Salter's Hall should be governed entirely by this consideration. *Mercurius Politicus*, April 1719, p. 246.

47. *Weekly Journal*, 18 October 1718, p. 579; 30 August 1718, p. 533.

48. *An Account of the Late Proceedings of the Dissenting Ministers of Salters-Hall* (London, 1719), p. 24.

49. *Serious Reflections*, p. 2.

50. See *Mercurius Politicus*, June 1718, pp. 338–41, 343, 418.

51. I must confess that living in Southern California, where earthquakes are almost routine, may influence my thoughts on this matter, but the earthquakes

of my dreams are very like the descriptions in *Robinson Crusoe*, while real earthquakes come so quickly that there is hardly time for terror. On the other hand, contemplation of the power of an earthquake would fit perfectly under what Burke describes as terror in categorizing it as the basic element in the sublime. See *An Essay on the Sublime and Beautiful*, in *The Works of Edmund Burke*, 8 vols. (London: George Bell, 1881), 1:88–89.

52. *Weekly Journal*, 20 December 1718, p. 15. Compare *Robinson Crusoe*, pp. 60, 62.

53. *Weekly Journal*, 20 January 1719, pp. 31–32; 24 January 1719, p. 44.

54. Ibid., 31 May 1718, p. 451; 21 June 1718, p. 475; 22 November 1718, p. 611; 31 May 1718, p. 458.

55. *Mercurius Politicus*, March 1719, pp. 172–73.

56. Ibid., November 1718, p. 697. In 1711 Defoe printed a letter, purportedly from Scotland, in which the correspondent complained of news reports from England listing so many suicides and asked Defoe if he was not right in thinking "that in your Nation of *England* there happens more self-Murthers, than in all Europe besides." See *Review*, ed. Arthur W. Secord (New York: Columbia University Press, 1937), 8:334–35.

57. See for example G. S. Starr's *Defoe and Casuistry* (Princeton: Princeton University Press, 1971), which proceeds on the grounds that the case for a complete religious interpretation has already been made.

58. Thoughts of imprisonment, particularly imprisonment for debt, were with Defoe since his early financial troubles, but never more than in December 1718, when, signing himself "Insolvent," he wrote a letter pointing out the absurdity of the creditor's position and the hopelessness of the imprisoned debtor's. "*These only*," he argued, "are condemned without Reprieve, without Possibility of Pardon or room for Escape." *Mercurius Politicus*, December 1718, pp. 756–57.

59. Neal Burnes and Douglas Kimura, "Isolation and Sensory Deprivation," in *Unusual Environments and Human Behavior* (Glencoe: Free Press, 1963), p. 169. This article summarizes many of the experiments with loneliness, isolation, and sensory deprivation conducted by John Lilly and others in connection with space flight as well as accounts of sailors and explorers from earlier periods. Many of their conclusions are not different from those of Roger Baynes in 1577, who ended his discussion of loneliness with the remark, "This *Solitarieness* of *place*, is therefore I say to be preferred unto *students*, and to such only as are thought to be *wise*." See *The Praise of Solitarinesse* (London: Francis Coldocke, 1577), p. 85.

60. Christopher Burney, *Solitary Confinement* (London: Macmillan, 1961), p. 8. See also Frieda Fromm-Reichman, "Loneliness," *Psychiatry* 22 (1959): 11.

61. Burney, *Solitary Confinement*, p. 4.

62. See Harry Slochower, *Mythopoesis* (Detroit: Wayne State University Press, 1970), pp. 5–23. He distinguishes four sections in the life of the mythic hero: (1) creation of an Eden (usually only a distant memory at the beginning); (2) the quest; (3) re-creation or homecoming; (4) tragic transcendence.

63. Mircea Eliade, *Rites and Symbols of Initiation*, trans. Willard R. Trask (New York: Harper and Row, 1975), p. 128.

64. For a discussion of Robinson Crusoe as a figure who merges with the tradition

of Ulysses, see Michael Seidel, *Epic Geography* (Princeton: Princeton University Press, 1976), pp. 97–104.

65. See Jean Jacques Rousseau, *Les Confessions*, ed. J. Voisine (Paris: Garnier Frères, 1964), pp. 348, 764.

66. John Bulkeley and John Cummins, *A Voyage to the South Seas in His Majesty's Ship the Wager in the Years 1740–1741*, ed. Arthur Howden Smith (New York: Robert M. McBride, 1927), especially pp. 95, 97.

67. Bachelard, *Poetics of Space*, pp. 69–70.

68. John Robert Moore argued briefly for the importance of contemporary events as a background for *Robinson Crusoe*, but he meant this in a more literal sense than my treatment of Defoe's responses to the daily happenings of his time as reported in the newspapers. To use the term "visionary" for Defoe is hardly inappropriate. The final section of his *Serious Reflections* is a "Vision," and throughout his life Defoe played with writing through the mask of a visionary or prophet. The majority of these exercises are in a comic form that might be called a mock-vision. See Moore, *Daniel Defoe, Citizen of the Modern World*, pp. 223–25.

Chapter 3

1. Sir Walter Scott, *On Novelists and Fiction*, ed. Ioan Williams (New York: Barnes and Noble, 1968), pp. 167–68.

2. See, for example, Paul Dottin, *Daniel Defoe et ses romans*, 3 vols. (Paris: Presses Universitaires, 1924), 3:582.

3. See J. H. Hexter, "Historiography: The Rhetoric of History," *International Encyclopedia of the Social Sciences*, ed. David L. Sills (New York: Macmillan, 1968); W. B. Gallie, "The Historical Understanding," *History and Theory* 3 (1964): 149–202; and Hayden White, *Metahistory* (Baltimore: Johns Hopkins University Press, 1973), pp. 1–42.

4. See Harold Toliver, *Animate Illusions* (Lincoln: University of Nebraska Press, 1974).

5. Herbert Butterfield, *The Historical Novel* (Cambridge: Cambridge University Press, 1924), pp. 70–71.

6. Ibid., p. 113.

7. Daniel Defoe, *Memoirs of a Cavalier* (Oxford: Blackwell, 1927), pp. 15–16. The page numbers of all subsequent references to this work will be included, in parenthesis, in the body of the text. I have also made use of information in other editions, particularly that edited by James T. Boulton (London: Oxford University Press, 1972).

8. Jean Le Clerc, *Life of the Famous Cardinal-Duke de Richelieu* (London: M. Gillyflower, 1695), 1:342. The center of unrest in 1630 was Dijon, but there were riots at Lyons in 1632. See André Steyert, *Nouvelle histoire de Lyon* (Lyon: Bernoux et Cumin, 1898–99), 3:256, and Boris Porchnev, *Les Soulèvements populaires en France de 1623 à 1648*, trans. Robert Mandrou (Paris: S.E.V.P.E.N., 1963), pp. 135–56.

9. See Arthur W. Secord, *Robert Drury's Journal and Other Studies* (Urbana: Uni-

versity of Illinois Press, 1961), pp. 72–133. Secord examines Defoe's sources and concludes that there are probably some yet undiscovered.

10. Daniel Defoe, *The Letters of Daniel Defoe*, ed. George H. Healey (Oxford: Clarendon Press, 1955), p. 135. Jan De Witt (1625–72), Dutch statesman, was caught by an outraged mob and killed.

11. Daniel Defoe, "Of the Carrying on of the Treaty in Scotland," *The History of the Union of Great Britain* (Edinburgh, 1709), p. 33.

12. Ibid., p. 64.

13. See La Mothe le Vayer, "Du peu de certitude qu'il y a dans l'histoire," *Oeuvres*, 7 vols. (Dresden: M. Groell, 1756–59), vol. 5, pt. 2: pp. 433–80.

14. James Boswell, *Life of Johnson*, ed. George B. Hill and L. F. Powell,, 6 vols. (Oxford: Clarendon Press, 1934–50), 2:195 (9 May 1775); 365 (18 April 1775).

15. John Dalrymple, *Memoirs of Great Britain and Ireland*, 4th ed., 3 vols. (Dublin: David Hay, 1773–88), 1:226. Johnson parodies Dalrymple's style in conversation with Boswell reported in *A Tour to the Hebrides*, ed. Frederick A. Pottle and Charles H. Bennett (London: Heinemann, 1936), pp. 391–93. I have selected a passage different from that parodied by Johnson to make Johnson's point more obvious for this paper.

16. See Donald Siebert, "Johnson and Hume on Miracles," *JHI* 36 (1975): 543–47.

17. Scott, *On Novelists and Fiction*, p. 167–68.

18. Daniel Defoe, *The Storm* (London, 1704), sig. A3^v.

19. Scott, *On Novelists and Fiction*, p. 169.

20. Arnaldo Momigliano, "Ancient History and the Antiquarian," in *Studies in Historiography* (New York: Harper and Row, 1966), pp. 20–21.

21. See Immanuel Kant, *On History*, ed. Lewis W. Beck (Indianapolis: Bobbs-Merrill, 1963), pp. 139–40; and compare Defoe's gloomy *Brief Deduction of the Original, Progress, and Immense Greatness of the British Woollen Manufacture* (London, 1727) with the optimistic *Plan of the English Commerce* (London, 1728). Defoe parodied the pessimism of Tory economics in the *Citizen*, 9 October 1727. For a good discussion of Kant's historical categories, see Frank E. Manuel, *Shapes of Philosophical History* (Stanford: Stanford University Press, 1967), pp. 70–91.

22. Scott, *On Novelists and Fiction*, p. 171.

23. Sir Walter Scott, *Old Mortality*, ed. Angus Calder (Hammondsworth: Penguin, 1975), pp. 16–17.

24. Defoe, "Of the Carrying on of the Treaty in Scotland," p. 56.

25. Defoe, "Minutes of the Parliament of Scotland with Observations Thereon," *History of the Union*, p. 73.

26. See A. R. Louch, "History as Narrative," *History and Theory* 8 (1969): 54–70. Louch's defense of narrative represents a strong apology for certain narrative features in history, but at no time does he abandon the didactic function of narrative: at no time is narrative defended as having some intrinsic value aside from its ability to substitute for experience and thereby make explanations more sound and forceful.

27. See Leonard Krieger, *The Politics of Discretion* (Chicago: University of Chicago Press, 1965), pp. 184–201; Defoe, "Of the Last Treaty," *History of the Union*, p.

3; "Of the Carrying on of the Treaty in Scotland," *History of the Union*, p. 1; Richard Steele, *Spectator*, no. 428.

28. Friedrich Nietzsche, *The Use and Abuse of History*, trans. Adrian Collins, 2d ed. rev. (Indianapolis: Bobbs-Merrill Co., 1957), pp. 16–17.

29. Michele Lifschitz, *Giambattista Vico*, quoted in Bruce Mazlish, *The Riddle of History* (New York: Harper and Row, 1966), p. 44.

30. See Maximillian Novak, introduction to *Of Captain Misson*, Augustan Reprint Society, no. 87 (Los Angeles: William Andrews Clark Memorial Library, 1961).

31. See, for example, Herbert G. Wright, "Defoe's Writings on Sweden," *RES* 16 (1940): 25–32.

32. *Present State of Europe* 31 (1720): 5.

33. Ibid., p. 23.

34. Ibid., p. 160.

35. Thomas Sherlock, *A Vindication of the Corporation and Test Acts* (London, 1718), p. 34.

36. Ibid., pp. 34–35.

37. Benjamin Hoadly, *The Common Rights of Subjects, Defended* (London, 1719), p. 168.

38. Thomas Sherlock, *An Answer to the Lord Bishop of Bangor's Late Book* (London, 1719), p. 11.

39. See James Peirce, *Some Reflections upon Dean Sherlock's Vindication of the Corporation and Test Acts*, 2d ed. (London, 1718), pp. 23–24.

40. Moses Lowman, *A Defence of the Protestant Dissenters* (London, 1718), pp. 12–13.

41. José Ortega y Gasset, *History as a System*, trans. Helene Weyl (New York: Norton, 1962), p. 212.

42. See, for example, Daniel Defoe, *The Manufacturer*, 9 March 1720.

43. Daniel Defoe, *A Letter to the Author of the Independent Whig* (London, 1720), title page.

44. Ibid., p. 12. Defoe attacks Sherlock by name, p. 27.

45. Ibid., p. 20.

46. Defoe's most important source, *The Swedish Intelligencer: The Second Part* (London, 1632), pp. 24–26, also printed Gustavus's moving speech warning his German troops against pillaging their own country. "I would rather ryde without Bootes," he stated, "then any wayes, or in the least degree, make my self the richer by the damage or undoing of these poor people" (pt. 3, p. 24). For examples of revolts among the peasants, see pt. 2, pp. 157, 178–79, 213.

47. La Mothe Le Vayer, *Oeuvres* 4:298, 315–16.

48. Scott, *On Novelists and Fiction*, p. 172.

49. See Frank E. Bastian, "Defoe's *Journal of the Plague Year* Reconsidered," *RES* 16 (1965): 151–73; and Everett Zimmerman, "H. F.'s Meditations: *A Journal of the Plague Year*," *PMLA* 87 (1972): 417–23.

50. *Daniel Defoe: Citizen of the Modern World* (Chicago: Chicago University Press, 1958), p. 320.

51. Samuel Pepys, *The Diary*, ed. Robert Latham and William Matthews, 9 vols. (Berkeley: University of California Press, 1970–76), 6:226, 342.

52. Walter G. Bell, *The Great Plague in London in 1665* (London: John Lane, 1924), pp. v–vii.

53. Daniel Defoe, *A Journal of the Plague Year* (London: Oxford University Press, 1969), p. xvi. All citations from this work in my text will refer to this edition.

54. Ainsworth makes Chowles, a coffin maker, and Judith, a nurse who robs and murders the victims of the plague, into his chief villains among the lower classes, and the Earl of Rochester and Sir Paul Parravicin his villains among the upper classes. He also depicts a riot led by a vicious leader of the mob named Barcroft. Defoe not only played down violence but tended to discount stories of murderous nurses.

55. See Nathaniel Hodge, *Loimologia*, 3d ed. (London, 1721), pp. 1–28, 131–36. The relationship of particular medical and psychological histories to fiction has long been recognized, and the same is true of individual case histories in sociological works like those of Oscar Lewis. But what is clear here is that medical, psychological, and sociological studies are aping fictional and dramatic forms. For some insights into this problem, see Steven Marcus, "Freud and Dora: Story, History, Case History," *Partisan Review* 41 (1971): 12–23, 89–108, particularly 20–22.

56. See Louch, "History as Narrative," *History and Theory*, pp. 54–57, for the historian's review.

57. Jorge Luis Borges, *Other Inquisitions, 1937–1952*, trans. Ruth L. C. Simms (Austin: University of Texas Press, 1964), p. 178.

58. Typical of Dekker's style is the following: "The World is our common Inne, in which wee haue no certaine abyding: It stands in the Road-way for all passengers. . . . A sicke-mans bed is the gate of first yard to this Inne, where death at our first arriuall stands like the Chamberlaine to bid you welcome, and is so bold, as to aske if you will alight, and he will shew you a Lodging" ("London Looke Backe," in *The Plague Pamphlets*, ed. F. P. Wilson [Oxford: Clarendon Press, 1925], pp. 182–83). Defoe's rejection of images like the dance of death is reminiscent of Dickens's refusal to get emotional mileage from such easy ironies. See Alexander Welsh, *The City of Dickens* (Oxford: Clarendon Press, 1971), p. 13.

59. Characters act out a dance of death masque that Rochester stages in St. Paul's. In William Harrison Ainsworth, *Historical Romances*, 20 vols. (Philadelphia: G. Barrie & Sons, n.d. [1890?]), 9:276–82.

60. Shortly after bringing this distinction to the attention of critics of the novel in his *The Sense of an Ending* (New York: Oxford University Press, 1967), p. 47, Frank Kermode made the tempting suggestion that there might be a close relationship between all kinds of narratives, not merely in fiction and history, but in writings in the social sciences as well. Kermode did not develop anything further from this speculation, but it ties in with efforts of writers like Jacques Derrida, who would like to see a form of history that is free from the tyranny of *chronos*. See Frank Kermode, "Novel, History and Type," *Novel* 1 (1968): 231–38, and Jacques Derrida, *Positions* (Paris: Editions de Minuit, 1972), pp. 76–82.

61. One of the objections that Georg Lukács made to some of the historical novels

of his contemporaries was the tendency of the authors to write fictional biographies in which the great historical figure assumed the central position in the work. The burden of history as the reader experiences it, he argued, should fall on the private individual—the fictional creation of the novelist. Without speaking specifically of *A Journal of the Plague Year*, Lukács praises Defoe, along with Fielding, Scott, Balzac, and Tolstoy, as writers who, without being Marxists, "grasped this living side of economy correctly and deeply," through having "deep ties with popular life in its most varied ramifications." He could not help appreciating the way Defoe portrayed the poor of London without making them appear as "a sociographically fixed species." See Georg Lukács, *The Historical Novel*, trans. Hannah and Stanley Mitchell (Lincoln: University of Nebraska Press, 1983), pp. 286–317.

62. See, for example, John Henry Raleigh, "Waverley as History," *Novel* 4 (1970): 14–29, and Peter D. Garside, "Scott and the 'Philosophical' Historians," *JHI* 36 (1975): 497–512. Much of this is based on the earlier work of Duncan Forbes.

63. Maximillian Novak, "Defoe and the Disordered City," *PMLA* 93 (1977): 241–52.

64. Gerhard von Rad, *Genesis*, trans. John H. Marks (London: SCM Press, 1970), p. 32. Alan C. Charity might classify this as a form of typology, but I find von Rad's comparison to saga more precise if less fashionable. See Alan C. Charity, *Events and Their Afterlife* (Cambridge: Cambridge University Press, 1966), pp. 1–4, 35–45, 80.

65. W. B. Gallie, *History and Theory* 3 (1964): 174.

66. I take this to be the point of Harold Toliver's *Animate Illusions*. See pp. 14–15, 388.

67. Giambattista Vico, *On the Study Methods of Our Times*, trans. Elio Gianturco (Indianapolis: Bobbs-Merrill, 1965), p. 43.

Chapter 4

1. Daniel Defoe, *The Fortunes and Misfortunes of Moll Flanders* (London: A. Swindells, n.d. [ca. 1750], p. 24.

2. George Borrow, *Works*, ed. Clement Shorter, 16 vols. (London: Constable, 1923), 3:324.

3. For this view of fairy tales, see Bruno Bettelheim, *The Uses of Enchantment* (New York: Vintage Books, 1976), pp. 132–36. Arguments against Bettelheim's varied readings of individual tales do not generally challenge this part of his thesis. See Eugen Weber, "The Reality of Folktales," *JHI* 42 (1981): 93–113.

4. John Sheppard was visited in his cell by admirers from all classes. See Daniel Defoe, *The History of the Remarkable Life of John Sheppard*, in *Romances and Narratives* by Daniel Defoe, ed. George Aitken, 16 vols. (London: Dent, 1895), 16:204–5.

5. (London: J. Pitts, n.d., [ca. 1810]). I quote from a copy in the New York Historical Society, Undated Ballads, "M." It was brought to my attention by Dr. Diane Dugaw.

6. Daniel Defoe, *The History of Laetitia Atkins* (London, 1776), pp. 277–78.

7. See above, p. 16.

8. Daniel Defoe, *Fortune's Fickle Distribution*, in a chapbook edition of *Moll Flanders* (London: n.p., 1730), p. 91.

9. Daniel Defoe, *The Fortunes and Misfortunes of Moll Flanders*, ed. G. S. Starr (London: Oxford University Press, 1971), p. 126. All subsequent references to this edition will appear in parentheses as part of the text.

10. *The Republican Bullies*, p. 6.

11. For my case for Defoe's irony, see "Conscious Irony in Moll Flanders," *College English* 26 (1964): 198–204.

12. Most picaresque fiction was, in its very nature, a secular version of spiritual autobiography, and the picaresque was the mode to which he was most directly indebted. For my objections to approaching *Moll Flanders* through spiritual autobiography, see my reviews of G. S. Starr's books, *Defoe and Spiritual Autobiography* (Princeton: Princeton University Press, 1965), in *JEGP* 66 (1967): 153–155, and *Defoe and Casuistry* (Princeton: Princeton University Press, 1971), in *Modern Language Quarterly* 33 (1972): 456–59. For the ingenious interpretation that Moll *thinks* she is writing a spiritual biography while actually writing a picaresque novel, see Richard Bjornson, *The Picaresque Hero* (Madison: University of Wisconsin Press, 1977), pp. 193–96.

13. Gerald Howson, "Who Was Moll Flanders?," *TLS* (18 January 1968): 63–64.

14. See Wayne Booth, *The Rhetoric of Fiction* (Chicago: University of Chicago Press, 1961), pp. 320–23. The best example of Defoe's sudden abandonment of an ironic posture at the very end of a work is *King William's Affection to the Church of England Examin'd* (London, 1703), p. 25.

15. See Ian Watt, "The Recent Critical Fortunes of Moll Flanders," *ECS* 1 (1967): 109–26.

16. That containing *The Compleat English Gentleman* and *Of Royall Educacion*, British Library Additional MSS 32, 555.

17. The tendency of a narrator to suggest moral positions in brief and often oversimplified phrases is part of the tradition of the picaresque from Alemán to Céline. Because I had previously approached Defoe's fiction more from the standpoint of content than technique, like Professor Ian Watt, I sometimes underestimated the very strong influence of picaresque fiction on Defoe's style.

18. A more obvious example of this type of dialogue through hints and suggestions may be found in the courtship scene with her Brother-Husband, pp. 91–93.

19. See my "Moll Flanders' First Love," *Papers of the Michigan Academy of Science, Arts, and Letters* 46 (1961): 635–43.

20. Daniel Defoe, *Moll Flanders*, ed. James Sutherland (Boston: Houghton Mifflin, 1959), p. 222.

21. See *The Fortunes and Misfortunes of Moll Flanders* (Birmingham: Joseph Russell, n.d.), p. 3. Some use *Clare* as a partial disguise of Defoe's original meaning, and others omit the name entirely.

22. A. A. Mendilow, *Time and the Novel* (New York: Humanities Press, 1965; reprint of 1952 ed.), pp. 91–94. For a reading of Moll Flanders in terms of the

split time perspective, see Everett Zimmerman, *Defoe and the Novel* (Berkeley: University of California Press, 1975), pp. 75–106; and for a somewhat different focus on time in this novel, see Paul Alkon, *Defoe and Fictional Time* (Athens: University of Georgia Press, 1979), pp. 110–32.

23. I agree with Everett Zimmerman's suggestion that "this man satisfies her only because she has deliberately restricted her feelings" (*Defoe and the Novel*, p. 87).

24. Daniel Defoe, *Condoling Letter to the Tatler* (London, 1710), pp. 13–14. For a numerological treatment of this passage, see Douglas Brooks, *Number and Pattern in the Eighteenth-Century Novel* (London: Routledge and Kegan Paul, 1973), pp. 47–48.

25. See Claude Lévi-Strauss, *Structural Anthropology*, trans. Claire Jacobson and Brooke Schoepf (New York: Doubleday, 1967), pp. 209–27.

26. For a further discussion of this point, see Chapter 5 of this study.

27. Franz Boas, *The Religion of the Kwakiutl Indians*, Columbia University Contributions to Anthropology, vol. 10 (New York: Columbia University Press, 1930), pt. 2, p. 5. Lévi-Strauss uses this story to illustrate the complex psychology of the shaman—his ability to believe even when he knows that much of his "fabulations of a reality" is "just a lie." See *Structural Anthropology*, p. 173.

28. "Defoe, Richardson, Joyce, and the Concept of Form in the Novel," in *Autobiography, Biography and the Novel*, by William Matthews and Ralph Rader (Los Angeles: William Andrews Clark Memorial Library, 1973), pp. 45–47.

29. G. S. Starr, *Defoe and Casuistry* (Princeton: Princeton University Press, 1971). Starr's able demonstration that the ethical arguments in Defoe's fiction could be linked to the interest in the application of various approaches to moral problems as it was fostered by Samuel Annesley during the Restoration has a number of implications for the study of Defoe's writings, not the least of which is to point up the relative sophistication of Defoe's background in dealing with speculative matters in ethics. My only major objection to Starr's treatment of casuistry is his implication that it involved a particular ideology rather than a method.

Chapter 5

1. *The Whore's Rhetorick* (New York: Ivan Oblensky, 1961; reprint of 1683 ed.), p. 135.

2. Alan McKillop, *The Early Masters of English Fiction* (Lawrence: University of Kansas Press, 1956), p. 38; Spiro Peterson, "The Matrimonial Theme of Defoe's *Roxana*," *PMLA* 70 (1955): 166–91; John Henry Raleigh, "Style and Structure and Their Import in Defoe's *Roxana*," *University of Kansas City Review* 20 (1953): 128–35. Peterson suggests that the complexity of *Roxana* might account for its unpopularity, but we should not forget that many critics found both *Moll Flanders* and *Roxana* shocking, and that *Roxana* was regarded as the more offensive of the two. "It [*Moll Flanders*] is not a book to be recommended to young readers," wrote William Trent in his anthology of Defoe; "perhaps it is not a book to be recommended to any one, which is one of the reasons why no

selections are given in the present volume from it or from *Roxana*" (*Daniel Defoe* [Indianapolis: Bobbs-Merrill, 1916], p. 215). See also Sir Walter Scott, "Daniel Defoe," in *Sir Walter Scott on Novelists and Fiction*, ed. Ioan Williams (New York: Barnes and Noble, 1968), pp. 167–68. David Higdon, "The Critical Fortunes and Misfortunes of Defoe's *Roxana*," *Bucknell Review* 20 (1972): 67–82; Douglas Brooks, *Number and Pattern in the Eighteenth-Century Novel* (London: Routledge and Kegan Paul, 1973), pp. 53–60; George Starr, *Defoe and Casuistry* (Princeton: Princeton University Press, 1972), pp. 165–89; John Richetti, *Defoe's Narratives* (New York: Oxford University Press, 1975), pp. 192–232.

3. Daniel Defoe, *Roxana* (New York: Popular Library, 1962).

4. For Defoe's division of the "Subject of Trade" into "Persons" and "Things," see *Review*, ed. Arthur Wellesley Secord (New York: Columbia University Press, 1938), 6 (21 June 1709): 135a. An interesting attempt to isolate pornographic elements in *Roxana* and *Moll Flanders* is LeRoy Smith's "Daniel Defoe: Incipient Pornographer," *Literature and Psychology* 22 (1972): 165–78.

5. Daniel Defoe, *Roxana: The Fortunate Mistress*, ed. Jane Jack (London: Oxford University Press, 1964), pp. 329–30. Subsequent references to this edition will be given parenthetically in the text.

6. Paul Dottin, *Daniel Defoe et ses romans* (Paris: Les Presses Universitaires, 1924), p. 731.

7. For a general discussion of Defoe's use of natural law, see my *Defoe and the Nature of Man* (Oxford: Clarendon, 1963). See also Robert Columbus, "Conscious Artistry in *Moll Flanders*," *SEL* 3 (1963): 426–28.

8. Columbus remarks on Moll's "very real relish for her seamy past," which is observable behind her pose of disapproval (pp. 416–18). Although Moll reveals a hatred for her past crimes and is genuinely repentant, her entire narrative is infused with a self-confidence and self-love that are inherent parts of her character. See Columbus, "Conscious Artistry," pp. 416–18, and my "Moll Flanders' First Love," *Papers of the Michigan Academy of Science, Arts, and Letters* 46 (1961): 635–43.

9. *Defoe's Narratives*, p. 201. For Roxana's method of enlisting the reader on her side in her ironies, see Starr, *Defoe and Casuistry*, p. 169.

10. See McKillop, *The Early Masters of English Fiction*, pp. 6–7.

11. Anthony Horneck, *The Happy Ascetick* (London, 1686), pp. 143–44. See also Daniel Defoe, *The Apparition of One Mrs. Veal*, in *The Fortunate Mistress*, Shakespeare Head ed., 14 vols. (Oxford: Blackwell, 1927), 2:239.

12. Daniel Defoe, *The Commentator*, no. 12 (8 February 1721).

13. Daniel Defoe, *Serious Reflections . . . of Robinson Crusoe*, in *Romances and Narratives by Daniel Defoe*, ed. George Aitken, 16 vols. (London: Dent, 1895), 3:247.

14. In *The Family Instructor* Defoe traced the career of a wicked son who dies in despair, "God having not pleased to grant him either the grace of repentance for his former sins, or to prevent future." See *The Novels and Miscellaneous Works of Daniel De Foe*, 20 vols. (Oxford: T. Tegg, 1840–41), 15:392 (373–93); cf. p. 21.

15. For a discussion of natural law on points of necessity, marriage, and grati-

tude, see Novak, *Defoe and the Nature of Man*, pp. 65–128. See also Samuel Pufendorf, *Of the Law of Nature and Nations*, trans. Basil Kennett (Oxford, 1703), pp. 90–92 (7. 1. 21–22), 199 (3. 6. 18).

16. For Defoe's theory of marriage as a voluntary contract, see *Robinson Crusoe*, Shakespeare Head ed., 14 vols. (Oxford: Blackwell, 1927), 3:19–21. See also *Review*, 2, *L. R.* (4 July 1705): 35, for Defoe's argument that bigamy was merely a violation of the laws of men, not of either the divine or natural law.

17. Roxana's belief that to sin against conscience was to double the sin was denied by many theologians. Jeremy Taylor wrote the "he that sins against a right and sure conscience, whatever the instance be, commits a great sin but not a double one," and Richard Baxter, admitting that it was "a very grievous aggravation of Sin," denied that such sins were unpardonable. See Jeremy Taylor, *Whole Works*, 10 vols. (London: Longman Green, 1862–65), 9:102; Richard Baxter, *Practical Works*, 4 vols. (London, 1707), 2:298–302, 912. See also Matthew Henry, *An Exposition of the Old and New Testament*, 6 vols. (New York: Robert Carter, n.d. [ca. 1850]), 5:245.

18. Defoe argued that where the individual conscience was convinced that an action was sinful, sin might be said to exist. His position was the same as that of William Ames, the great Puritan moralist whose writings were used in the dissenting academy that Defoe attended. Ames argued that "he alwaies sinneth who does any thing against conscience: but if the conscience doth not erre, but the thing is as erroneous conscience supposeth, then he sinneth doubly. First, in doing that which is il in it selfe; and secondly, in doing it after an evil manner" (*Conscience* [London, 1643], p. 9 [1. 4. 6]).

19. Daniel Defoe, *A Collection of Miscellany Letters out of Mist's Weekly Journal*, 4 vols. (London, 1722–27), 3:15.

20. Paul Dottin argued that Defoe was attempting to use the mannerisms of this genre, but that he was "trop puritain pour imiter ces livres frivoles" (*Daniel De Foe*, 3:719), but John Richetti suggests that Defoe deliberately reversed the literary conventions of the contemporary novel. See *Defoe's Narratives*, p. 215. For a similar attitude in a contemporary romance, see Eliza Haywood's *Idalia or The Unfortunate Mistress*, 3 pts. in 1 vol. (London, 1723), pt. 1, p. 57.

21. Cf. Saint Evremond, *Works*, trans. Pierre Desmaizeaux (London, 1728), 2:77; and Defoe, *Review* 1 (20 January 1705): 381a; 1 (23 January 1705): 387b; 2, *L.R.* (13 June 1705): 2.

22. For Defoe's view of gratitude, see William Lee, *Daniel Defoe: His Life and Recently Discovered Writings*, 3 vols. (London: John Hotten, 1869), 3:345. For the idea that willful sin was an act of ingratitude to God, see John Calvin, *Works*, vol. 39, trans. John Owen, 52 vols. (Edinburgh: Calvin Translation Society, 1849), 38:76; Thomas Becon, *Early Works* (Cambridge: Cambridge University Press, 1843), p. 185; John Tillotson, *Works*, ed. Ralph Baker, 2 vols. (London, 1712), 2:47.

23. Robert South, *Sermons*, 4 vols. (Philadelphia: Sorin & Ball, 1845), 1:286. South associates luring others into sin with the worst of sins—taking pleasure in sin itself (Romans 1:32). Defoe recommended the sermons of South and Tillotson in *The Protestant Monastery* (London, 1727 [1726]), p. 30. See also Peterson's

remarks on the social significance in the corruption of the maid by the Mistress ("The Matrimonial Theme of Defoe's *Roxana*," pp. 176–81).

24. See Walter Wilson, *Memoirs of the Life and Times of Daniel De Foe*, 3 vols. (London: Hurst, Chance & Co., 1830), 3:528–32; William Lee, *Daniel Defoe: His Life and Recently Discovered Writings*, 1:373–74; and William Minto, *Daniel Defoe* (London: Macmillan, 1879), p. 154. Probably the best judgments on *Roxana* are John Robert Moore's suggestions that she is "Moll's opposite number in Defoe's gallery of women," and Spiro Peterson's interesting suggestion that *Moll Flanders* and *Roxana* can be considered as a "sequence-novel" on the theme of "wife and whore." See John Robert Moore, *Daniel Defoe* (Chicago: University of Chicago Press, 1958), p. 245, and Spiro Peterson, "The Matrimonial Theme of Defoe's *Roxana*," p. 167.

25. Lee, *Defoe*, 3:349–50. Peterson remarks that as "Roxana passed from the state of unfortunate wife to that of fortunate mistress, she altered in character from a passive victim to a diabolic agent of evil" ("The Matrimonial Theme of Defoe's *Roxana*," p. 175).

26. Cf. Lee, *Defoe*, 2:501, and Daniel Defoe, *The Political History of the Devil* (London, 1726), p. 235. Defoe substitutes the more traditional sin of pride for Young's "Love of Fame."

27. Defoe, *The Political History of the Devil*, p. 335. See also John Collins, "Sermons," Huntington Library, Unaccessioned MS, fols. 44–46. In his sermon of 26 March 1681, Collins made a lengthy comparison between the fallen Adam and Satan. Defoe took down these sermons in his own hand at a time when he was contemplating becoming a dissenting minister. That he continued to admire Collins is evidenced by the presence of Collins's name in his list of the best preachers among dissenting clergymen. See *The Present State of the Parties in Great Britain* (London, 1712), p. 352.

28. This is a traditional grouping. See Richard Baxter, *Practical Works*, 2:886. For the sins that arise from her vanity, see the discussion of luxury in my *Economics and the Fiction of Daniel Defoe* (Berkeley: University of California Press, 1962), pp. 134–39.

29. See Novak, "Moll Flanders' First Love," pp. 635–43.

30. The arguments she offers may be connected with the Jesuits' doctrines of "probability" and "directing the intention." See Blaise Pascal, *Pensées and the Provincial Letters*, trans. Thomas M'Crie, Modern Library ed. (New York: Random House, 1941), pp. 377–78, 404, 439–49. See also Haywood, *Idalia*, 2:55, for the theory that "there are no Rules, alas! to limit Love."

31. In a different context, Defoe would have concurred with Roxana's attack on contemporary marriage as a form of slavery for women, and her argument has a certain force even here. I agree with Richetti (*Defoe's Narratives*, p. 224), however, that at this point in the novel the argument is mainly an indication of Roxana's will to power. Sir Robert Clayton is amused by Roxana's "Amazonian" attitude toward marriage and money, but Samuel Pufendorf called such feminist behavior "Barbarous at least, if not Beastly," and Pierre Bayle, conceding that Amazonian marriages were common throughout the world, suggested that, as far as Europe was concerned, "Things are very well as they

are." See Pufendorf, *Law of Nature*, p. 78 (6. 1. 9), and Pierre Bayle, *The Dictionary*, trans. Pierre Desmaizeaux, 2d ed., 5 vols. (London, 1734), 5:31. Defoe attacked Roxana's attitude as an inversion of the natural order of the sexes (*Review* 1 [27 January 1702]: 392a). Professor James Sutherland has suggested to me that Defoe may have been drawing on "The History of the Life and Memoirs of Mrs. Behn" for some of Roxana's attitudes toward marriage and her Dutch lover. Some of the incidents are similar, and there may even be some verbal borrowing. See *All the Histories and Novels Written by the Late Ingenious Mrs. Behn*, ed. Charles Gildon, 4th ed. (London, 1700), pp. v–viii. For Defoe's attack on the vices of Charles II's court and especially the masquerades and dancing, see *Fears of the Pretender Turn'd into the Fears of Debauchery* (London, 1715), p. 32. See pp. 116–17 below for the ways in which the court of Charles II is a reflection of the court of the reigning monarch, George I.

32. *The Fortunate Mistress*, 2:49. Defoe seems to have been thinking of Locke's definition of madness: "if either by any sudden very strong impression, or long fixing his fancy upon one sort of thoughts, incoherent ideas have been cemented together so powerfully, as to remain united," the victim may be made "frantic" or put into a disordered condition. See John Locke, *An Essay Concerning Human Understanding*, ed. Alexander Fraser, 2 vols. in 1 (New York: Dover, 1950), 1:209–10.

33. Defoe, *Serious Reflections*, p. 62. Robert South described the failure of parents to provide a good example for their children as a most "unnatural" act: "For certainly, where a child finds his own parents his perverters he cannot so properly be said to be born as to be damned in the world" (1:283–84).

34. Daniel Defoe, *The Shortest Way with the Dissenters* (Oxford: Blackwell, 1927), pp. 2–6. See also Peterson, "The Matrimonial Theme of Defoe's *Roxana*," pp. 176–81, for the social implications of Roxana's career.

35. For the view that Amy and Susan represent rival claims on Roxana and that Roxana's rage against Amy is a displacement for her rage against her daughter, see Everett Zimmerman, *Defoe and the Novel* (Berkeley: University of California Press, 1975), p. 169.

36. Daniel Defoe, *The Wickedness of a Disregard to Oaths* (London, 1723), p. 26.

37. Lee, *Defoe*, 3:179.

38. Jonathan Bishop, "Knowledge, Action, and Interpretation in Defoe's Novels," *JHI* 13 (1952): 11.

39. Daniel Defoe, *An Apology for the Army* (London, 1715), p. 15; Benjamin Boyce, "The Question of Emotion in Defoe," *SP* 50 (1953): 44–58. For a brief discussion of courage in Defoe's fiction, see Arthur Wellesley Secord, *Studies in the Narrative Method of Defoe* (Urbana: University of Illinois Press, 1924), pp. 221–22.

40. Daniel Defoe, *Review* 8 (17 May 1712): 721.

41. Cf. Pufendorf, *Law of Nature*, p. 131 (2. 4. 12); and Defoe, *Review* 8 (17 May 1712): 722a.

42. See Willa Cather, *On Writing* (New York: Knopf, 1953), pp. 83–85, and Ernest Baker, *The History of the English Novel*, 10 vols. (London: H. F. & G. Witherly, 1924–39), 3:196. John Henry Raleigh describes the "antiseptic" language in which Roxana speaks of her love affairs, but fails to connect the language with

Roxana's attitude toward love. See "Style and Structure . . . in Defoe's *Roxana*," p. 134. William Ames described the "benummed Conscience" and the "*stupidity*" of the hardened sinner: "A *stupide Conscience* is that, which doth not its office in *accusing* and *condemning*, unless it be for the *greatest sinnes*, and when it is forced by most *grievous Judgements*. For like as men sicke of a *Lethargie* or *Drowsinesse*, are not wakened commonly, unlesse it be through some great noise: so likewise this conscience is not moved, unlesse it be by the thunder of Gods Judgements" (*Conscience*, p. 28 [1. 15. 1–7]). See also Collins, "Sermons," fol. 49.

43. For a list of Defoe's heroic virtues, see *Rogue's on Both Sides* (London, 1711), p. 30.

44. See *Serious Reflections*, p. 266; and *Commentator*, no. 46 (10 June 1720).

45. See *Captain Singleton*, ed. Shiv Kumar (London: Oxford University Press, 1969), p. 269, and Lee, *Defoe*, 3:110–13.

46. Daniel Defoe, *Essay on the History and Reality of Apparitions* (London, 1727), pp. 104–11. Defoe scored the margin next to Collins's remark that true repentance was accompanied by a sense of "Rest." "Take care therefore," wrote Collins, "least you wipe of those teares from your Eyes, before Christ hath haken the Sin off from your hearts" (fol. 167).

47. *Serious Reflections*, pp. 24, 63.

48. Daniel Defoe, *More Reformation*, in *A Second Volume of the Writings of the Author of the True-Born Englishman* (London, 1705), p. 36. In light of Defoe's refusal to continue the career of Roxana, it is interesting to compare his refusal to dwell on the "Horrid wickedness" of Jonathan Wild, who is transformed into a "devil incarnate" and dies impenitent on the scaffold. See *The Life and Actions of Jonathan Wild*, in *Romances and Narratives by Daniel Defoe*, 16:27a. See also *The Family Instructor*, pp. 392–93, and *Mercurius Politicus*, February 1717, p. 112, where Defoe praised *A Letter from Mr. Burdett*, a pamphlet in which the narrator is a condemned murderer who lacks "the grace of repentance."

49. See Defoe's attack on the grand tour to Italy in *A New Family Instructor* (London, 1727), p. 17.

50. Ian Watt, "The Naming of Characters in Defoe, Richardson, and Fielding," *RES* 25 (1949): 322–38. Defoe, who frequently quoted from Plutarch's *Lives* and especially the life of Alexander, would have thought primarily of the wicked Roxana who captivated Alexander by her dancing and murdered his queen, Statira, in a fit of jealousy.

51. Anthony Hamilton, *Memoirs of the Life of Count de Grammont*, trans. Abel Boyer (London, 1714), p. 246.

52. Richard Head and Francis Kirkman, *The English Rogue* (London: n.p., 1874?), 2:355.

53. *The English Rogue*, 2:356.

54. Paul Dottin suggests Mrs. Barry and Mary Wortley Montagu as possible candidates. Mademoiselle Bardou is John Robert Moore's suggestion. See Paul Dottin, "Les Sources de la *Roxana* de Daniel De Foe," *Revue Anglo-Americaine* 4 (1927): 531–34, and John Robert Moore, *Defoe in the Pillory and Other Studies*, Indiana University Humanities Series no. 1 (Bloomington: Indiana University Press, 1939), p. 43.

55. If Defoe surrounds Roxana's decision to yield to the entreaties of her Landlord with numerous moral arguments for and against from Amy, the Landlord, and Roxana herself, the decision of Louise de Keroualle, afterward Duchess of Portsmouth, was often treated with considerable levity and sarcasm. The author of *The Secret History of the Reigns of Charles II and James II* (1690), p. 23, remarked on the mock ceremony that it was "A thing in some measure justifiable in a Prince, since the Law allows all Men one Wife; and therefore a King, who is above Law may surely have two." Although Louise may have tried to convince herself that she was truly married to Charles, the atmosphere surrounding the "marriage" must have resembled that of a masquerade.

56. "Rochester's Farewell," in *Poems*, ed. Vivian de Sola Pinto (London: Routledge, 1953), pp. 153–54. See also Saint Evremond, *Works*, 2:318–22; and Laurence Echard, *The History of England* (London, 1720), p. 923.

57. In Richard Knolles, *The General Historie of the Turkes* (London, 1638), p. 759. For Defoe's knowledge of "the She-Comedian, who acted *Roxellana*," see *Remarks on the Speeches of William Paul Clerk, and John Hall of Otterburn, Esq.* (London, 1716), p. 8. Defoe's knowledge of Knolles's work goes back to 1682, when Defoe drew upon it for his "Historical Collections."

58. For information on Hester Davenport, see John Harold Wilson, *All the King's Ladies* (Chicago: University of Chicago Press, 1958), pp. 137–39. A performance of *Mustapha* in 1666 witnessed by John Evelyn made him think once more of "Roxalana . . . the E. of Oxfords Misse" (*Diary*, ed. E. S. de Beer [Oxford: Clarendon Press, 1955], 3:309, 465–66). Everett Zimmerman speaks forcefully of Roxana's authoritarian streak in dealing with her children, and Defoe may have associated this with Roxana's knowledge of Turkish manners. See Zimmerman, *Defoe and the Novel*, p. 165.

59. Charles Johnson's *Sultaness*, a translation of Racine's play, was staged in 1717 and printed with a frontispiece in which Racine's heroine is wearing a costume not very different from that used in the frontispiece to *Roxana*. Defoe may have read the *Persian Letters*. See *A Collection of Miscellany Letters*, 3:130. For a discussion of Roxana as a stage type, see Lucyle Hook, "Shakespeare Improv'd; or, A Case for the Affirmative," *Shakespeare Quarterly* 4 (1953): 291–93.

60. Daniel Defoe, *A Treatise Concerning the Use and Abuse of the Marriage Bed* (London, 1727), p. 317. For Defoe's attitude toward primitivism, see Novak, *Defoe and the Nature of Man*, pp. 36–50.

61. Some questions have been raised about any relationship between the court of Charles II and *Roxana*. David Higdon (emphatically) and Rodney Baine (with reservations) have argued that the title page, with its reference to "the Person known by the Name of the Lady Roxana in the time of Charles II," must be ignored in the name of what would otherwise be a neat time scheme. Higdon carefully diagrams Roxana's life from her birth in 1673 to the point at which she might be writing her memoirs some years after 1724, the actual year when the novel was published. Unfortunately, the notion of a novel published in 1724 being written three to five years after that date is as mind boggling as her presence in the court of Charles II as a courtesan when, if her opening statements are to be credited, she was an infant. David Blewitt, beginning with my

original suggestion that Defoe was reflecting on his own era through his picture of the Restoration, shows conclusively that Defoe's remarks on masquerades and disguise applied vividly to the period of the 1720s in which the masquerade impresario, John James Heidegger, flourished. But Blewitt refuses to abandon the Restoration as Defoe's chronological center and concludes with excellent good sense and in complete violation of all logic that Defoe intended to describe both periods *"at the same time."* Recently, Paul Alkon has agreed with Blewitt and raised questions about the necessity for a realistic time scheme in fiction. See Higdon, "Critical Fortunes and Misfortunes of Roxana," pp. 71–77; Baine, "Roxana's Georgian Setting," *SEL* 15 (1975): 459–72; Blewitt, "'Roxana' and the Masquerades," *MLR* 65 (1970): 499–502; *Defoe's Art of Fiction* (Toronto: University of Toronto Press, 1979), pp. 124–127; and Alkon, *Defoe and Fictional Time* (Athens: University of Georgia Press, 1979), pp. 53–58.

62. See Baine's discussion of Defoe's "protective ambiguity" in "Roxana's Georgian Setting," p. 468.

63. *A System of Magic*, in *The Novels and Miscellaneous Works of De Foe*, 12:331–32. Cf. *Alexander Bendo's Bill*, quoted in Vivian de Sola Pinto, *Rochester* (London: John Lane, 1935), pp. 105–10.

64. *A Collection of Miscellany Letters*, 4:176.

65. Cf. Daniel Defoe, *Review* 5 (1 March 1709): 577; and *An Essay upon Projects*, in *The Earlier Life and Chief Earlier Works of Daniel Defoe*, ed. Henry Morley (London: Routledge, 1889), p. 147; Pufendorf, *Law of Nature*, pp. 100–101 (6. 1. 31); Pierre Bayle, *Dictionary*, 3:814a; Bernard Mandeville, *The Fable of the Bees*, ed. F. B. Kaye (Oxford: Clarendon Press, 1957), 1:64–65.

66. For another view of the question of disguise and identity in *Roxana*, see Zimmerman, *Defoe and the Novel*, pp. 156–64.

67. Bonamy Dobrée, *English Literature in the Early Eighteenth Century* (New York: Clarendon Press, 1959), p. 429.

68. Robert Hume, "The Conclusion of Defoe's *Roxana*," *ECS* 3 (1970): 490.

69. Dottin, *De Foe*, p. 731; Dobrée, *English Literature in the Early Eighteenth Century*, p. 425; McKillop, *The Early Masters of English Fiction*, p. 37; Boyce, "The Question of Emotion," pp. 55–58.

70. For Defoe's theory of the use of fiction, see *Review* 7 (11 April 1710): 25; *A New Family Instructor*, pp. 52–53; and *A Collection of Miscellany Letters*, 4:210.

71. *The Family Instructor*, p. 392. See also *The History and Reality of Apparitions*, in *The Novels and Miscellaneous Works of De Foe*, 13:43.

72. The distinction between the "seriousness" of Defoe's themes and the seriousness of "imaginative truth" is probably the major modern objection to Defoe. See Jane Jack, quoted in Dobrée, *English Literature in the Early Eighteenth Century*, p. 430.

Chapter 6

1. Daniel Defoe, *Jonathan Wild* (London, 1725), p. iv.

2. See especially Ernest Bernbaum, *The Mary Carleton Narratives, 1663–1673* (Cambridge: Harvard University Press, 1914), pp. 78–100.

3. For Lamb's comments, see Walter Wilson, *Memoirs of the Life and Times of Daniel De Foe*, 3 vols. (London: Hurst, Chance & Co., 1830), 3:428.

4. For a typical response to Rembrandt and realism in picture and prose fiction, see Lenglet-Dufresnoy, *De l'usage des romans*, 2 vols. (Amsterdam, 1734), 1:198.

5. Edmund Burke, *A Philosophical Enquiry into the Origin of Our Ideas on the Sublime and Beautiful*, ed. J. T. Boulton (Notre Dame: University of Notre Dame Press, 1968), p. 47.

6. *Tryals for High Treason and Other Crimes* (London, 1720), p. x.

7. *The Innocent Mistress* (London, 1697), p. 42 (5. 2). For a similar and equally typical title, see *An Account of a Most Horrid and Barbarous Murther and Robbery Committed on the Body of Captain Brown* (London, 1694).

8. *God's Revenge against the Abominable Sin of Adultery* (London, 1679), p. 182.

9. Ibid., p. 167.

10. Ibid., p. 177.

11. Published between 1665 and 1671, this collection of adventures is an odd mixture of the picaresque and jestbook tradition. It draws its morality from the English libertine movement, then at its peak, and permits its witty rogues to commit any crime, including murder, without hint of punishment. When George Borrow complained that Newgate Calendars "have usually been compiled in language, which sympathized and accorded with their subject," he was exaggerating, but the description is right enough for *The English Rogue*. See *Celebrated Trials*, ed. George Borrow (London, 1825), p. iii, and Ronald Paulson, *Popular Art in the Age of Fielding and Hogarth* (Notre Dame: University of Notre Dame Press, 1979), p. 18.

12. Michel Foucault, *Discipline and Punish*, trans. Alan Sheridan (New York: Vintage Books, 1979), pp. 87–88.

13. See Alexander Smith, *A Complete History of the Lives and Robberies of the Most Notorious Highwaymen*, ed. Arthur Hayward (London: George Routledge, 1933), p. 108. For examples of the description of Newgate as a subgenre, see T. H., *A Glimpse of Hell; or, A Short Description of the Common Side of Newgate* (London, 1704), and *The History of the Press Yard* (London, 1717).

14. Smith, *A Complete History*, p. 290. For a partial list of Smith's sources, see Robert Singleton, "English Criminal Biography, 1651–1722," *Harvard Library Bulletin* 18 (1970): 71, n. 19.

15. Smith, *A Complete History*, p. 337. See also Congden's speech to a former pirate, p. 338.

16. Smith, *A Complete History*, p. 451.

17. *Weekly Journal or Saturday's Post*, 16 September 1721.

18. *The Tryal and Condemnation of Arundel Coke* (London, 1722), p. 15.

19. Daniel Defoe, *A General History of the Pirates*, ed. Manuel Schonhorn (London: Dent, 1972), p. 134. For a general discussion of this theme, see my *Economics and the Fiction of Daniel Defoe* (Berkeley: University of California Press, 1962), pp. 102–127.

20. Colonel Jack was not the first character to receive such treatment. The "Spanish Rogue," Guzman de Alfarache, the fictional creation of Mateo Alemán, was often considered a real character, and a number of picaresque novels

appear to be a mixture of real adventures and fictions. In all such cases, however, the influence and literary pressure is on autobiography or biography as the form that must be made to resemble the fictional form (the picaresque). The same pressure exists in the Newgate Calendars, and Defoe's particular type of picaresque fiction exerted a specific kind of influence on criminal biography. For a reading that reverses the flow of influence, see Ralph Rader, "Defoe, Richardson, Joyce and the Concept of the Novel," *Autobiography, Biography and the Novel* (Los Angeles: William Andrews Clark Memorial Library, 1973), pp. 40–47.

21. Thomas Salmon published *A Critical Review of the State Trials* (London, 1737) devoted, at least nominally, to emphasizing the legal precedents in the proceedings, but from the start trials were regarded as entertainment. In a four-volume abridgment of the thirty-three volumes of *A Compleat Collection of State Trials* edited by T. B. and T. H. Howell and published in 1816 and 117, H. L. Stephen speaks of the "charm" of the Howell collection and considers himself in competition with Scott and other historical novelists for readers. One writer (Henry Bliss) even versified a volume of trials in 1833.

22. Thomas Salmon is sometimes suggested as the likely editor of the collections of 1719 and 1720, but he appears to speak of a different editor. See Salmon, *A Critical Review of the State Trials*, p. iii.

23. *Tryals for High Treason*, 1:vii.

24. In *The Tryal of Spenser Cowper . . .* (London, 1741), pp. 777–78.

25. Andrew Knapp and William Baldwin, *The Newgate Calendar*, 4 vols. (London: J. Robins, 1825), 2:385. The case became part of various *Newgate Calendars* shortly after the trial in 1768.

26. Samuel Richardson, *Clarissa*, Everyman Library ed., 4 vols. (London: Dent, 1932), 2:420–23. See his belief that the "law was not made for such a man as me" (2:267).

27. Ian Watt, *The Rise of the Novel* (Berkeley: University of California Press, 1957), p. 173.

28. Knapp and Baldwin, *The Newgate Calendar*, 2:246. See also the accounts in *The New Newgate Calendar*, 5 vols. (London: A. Hogg, 1779–84), 4:131–47 and Eric Watson, *Eugene Aram* (Toronto: Canada Law Book Co., 1913), passim.

29. David Hume had argued that continued identity was merely a mental fiction, and while John Locke had been more restrained, he too placed identity in the operation of the mind. See David Hume, *A Treatise of Human Nature*, ed. L. A. Selby-Bigge (Oxford: Clarendon, 1896), pp. 189–202, 259–63, and John Locke, *An Essay Concerning Human Understanding*, ed. Alexander Fraser, 2 vols. in 1 (New York: Dover Publications, 1959), 1:447–70.

30. Alexander Welsh, "Realism as a Practical and Cosmic Joke," *Novel* 9 (1975): 23–29.

31. Compare William Godwin, *Caleb Williams*, ed. David McCracken (London: Oxford University Press, 1970), pp. 216, 220; and Defoe, *History of the Pirates*, p. 394. The entire conduct of Raymond in relation to democratic procedure among the thieves parallels that of Misson.

32. See particularly George Rudé, *Wilkes and Liberty* (Oxford: Clarendon, 1962). For a discussion of the social implications of the Black Acts, see E. P. Thomp-

son, *Whigs and Hunters* (New York: Pantheon, 1975), especially pp. 81–115 and 190–218.

33. Dogan and Murphy were members of the "coal-heavers gang" and were attempting to strike for an increase in wages. See Knapp and Baldwin, *The Newgate Calendars*, 2:406. Melville's *Billy Budd*, set at the end of the eighteenth century, is an obvious example of an innocent man executed to maintain the principles of justice during a time of public disorder.

34. See my "The Disordered City," *PMLA* 92 (1977): 241–52.

35. *The New Newgate Calendar*, 5:75.

36. Georg Lukács, *The Historical Novel*, trans. Hannah and Stanley Mitchell (Boston: Beacon Press, 1963), pp. 21–28, 36–45.

Index

178   Index

Mist, Nathaniel, 25, 77
Mist's Weekly Journal. See Defoe,
  Daniel, Weekly Journal
Mode, xiv–xv
Moll, Herman, 77
Momigliano, Arnaldo, 53
Money, 20, 27, 108, 128, 151 n. 14
Montesquieu, Charles Louis de Sec-
  ondat, Baron de, 116
Moore, John Robert, xv, 18, 25, 65,
  66, 109, 154 n. 68, 163 n. 24, 165
  n. 54
Moore, Marianne, 27
Morality, 6, 16, 78, 86, 88, 100, 101,
  113–17 passim, 119, 124, 159
  n. 17, 168 n. 11
Morgan, Henry, 126
Murder, 27, 39, 52, 87, 100, 108,
  109, 110, 112, 116, 119, 124,
  130–32, 133, 134, 137, 138, 139,
  144, 145, 165 n. 48, 168 n. 11
Murphy, James, 142
Myth, xiv, 9, 10–17, 21, 45–46, 55,
  72, 75, 77, 91, 99–120, 131, 145,
  149 n. 28, 153 n. 62
Mythology, Greco-Roman, 15

Names of characters, 113, 115, 116
Narrative, 19, 21, 54, 70, 76, 77, 121,
  123, 124, 126, 132, 133, 134, 141,
  145, 155 n. 26, 157 n. 60
Natural disasters, 31–34, 41–42, 53,
  54, 55
Nature, 11, 31, 110
Newgate Calendar, 21, 126, 127,
  131–38 passim, 140–45 passim, 168
  n. 11, 169 nn. 20, 28, 170 nn. 33,
  35
Nietzsche, Frederich, 55
Noailles, Cardinal, 40
Nochlin, Linda, 9
Novak, Maximillian, 84
Novel, xv, 21, 37, 46, 133, 142, 145,
  157 nn. 60, 61, 168 n. 20; history
  of, see Fiction, history of; origins
  of, 4; of manners, xv, 5

Oades, William, 29
Oakeshott, Michael, 11
Ortega y Gasset, José, 59
Overbury, Sir Thomas, 133
Ovid, 114

Painting, 1, 31, 122
Palatine, Elector, 57, 58
Pascal, Blaise, 163 n. 30
Passions in art, 2
Passivity, 110–11
Paulson, Ronald, 126
Peirce, James, 59
Pepys, Samuel, 65
Peterson, Spiro, 99, 160 n. 2, 162
  n. 23, 163 nn. 24, 25
Peter the Great (Czar of Russia), 28,
  29
Picaresque, 5, 6, 8, 77, 95, 124, 126,
  159 n. 12, 168 nn. 11, 20
Piracy, 13, 32, 33, 37, 73, 126,
  130–31, 151
Pix, Mary, 124, 125
Plagues, 31, 59, 64–68, 69, 129,
  144–45, 157 nn. 52–55, 58
Plutarch, 19, 165 n. 50
Politics, xii, 15, 16, 17, 25, 50, 57,
  122, 132, 134, 141
Polyandry, 115
Polygamy, 115
Pope, Alexander, xi, xii
Poverty, 8, 54, 73, 90, 102, 106, 107
Presbyterians, 7, 51, 54, 152 n. 41
Present State of Europe, The, 57
Pride, 106, 107, 118
Primitivism, 116
Prison. See Imprisonment
Property, 15, 144
Prostitution, 8, 73, 83, 84, 87–88, 89,
  99, 100, 101, 103, 105–8 passim,
  111, 113–17 passim, 139–41
Protestants, 13, 15, 40, 56–57, 58,
  63, 65, 115
Providence, 21, 45, 53, 55, 112
Psychology, 5, 16, 44, 45, 52, 65, 87,
  89, 90, 91, 100, 110, 120, 157 n. 55